D1555535

INSTITUTIONALIZING LITERACY

The Historical Role of College Entrance Examinations in English

MARY TRACHSEL

Southern Illinois University Press
Carbondale and Edwardsville

Library of Congress Cataloging-in-Publication Data

Trachsel, Mary, 1953–
    Institutionalizing literacy : the historical role of college
entrance examinations in English / Mary Trachsel.
        p.   cm.
    Includes bibliographical references (p.) and index.
    1. English philology—Study and teaching—United States—History.
2. Universities and colleges—United States—Entrance examinations—
History. 3. English Philology—Examinations—History.
4. Literacy—United States—History.   I. Title.
PE68.U5T73   1992
420'.76—dc20   91-23981
ISBN 0-8093-1732-X   CIP

The paper used in this publication meets the minimum
requirements of American National Standard for Information
Sciences—Permanence of Paper for Printed Library Materials,
ANSI Z39.48-1984. ∞

Contents

Preface

The field of composition studies has responded eagerly to a recent explosion of research and theory on the subject of literacy, invoking that body of scholarship to inform composition theory as well as pedagogy. In embracing literacy as its area of professional expertise, writing instruction stakes its claim in the very center of the academic curriculum, for as the opening sentence of *Rhetoric and Reality,* James Berlin's study of writing instruction in American colleges in the twentieth century, maintains, "Literacy has always and everywhere been the center of the educational enterprise" (1).

Curious as to why a concept presumably so essential to the institutional mission of the academy should be relegated almost exclusively to composition studies, a relatively disempowered segment of the discipline of English studies, I began this book as an attempt to trace the evolution of the academy's construction of literacy. In piecing together the historical development of the concept, I have focused my attention on the record of college entrance examinations, convinced that any attempt to measure or assess literacy skills must be grounded in a definition of literacy itself. What I have discovered in the process of examining those documents, along with a good bit of printed discourse surrounding their formulation and use, is a gradual but steadily intensifying cleavage of English studies as it has struggled to meet certain fundamental demands of professionalization.

On the surface, the separate disciplinary divisions resulting from this cleavage can be identified as reading—or literary studies—on the one hand, and writing—or composition studies—on the other. But as the historical narrative emerging from the pages of this book reveals, underlying the surface manifestations of disciplinary fragmentation are philosophical and traditional conflicts that constitute an intradisciplinary dialogue concerning the social and cultural mission of the American academy, the professional status of English studies and its position within the academic curriculum, and the influences of an increasingly corporate and bureaucratic capitalist economy on the shaping of academic disciplines.

In the early stages of the historical account offered in this book, the use of entrance examinations to define the parameters of disciplinary expertise seems obvious. The first entrance exams in English, like those of other academic departments, were produced by academic specialists—a small number of individual professors who saw the exams as a medium for the articulation of their expectations for the academic preparation in their field that would qualify an applicant as "college material." Because such exams formed the basis by which individuals could be included or excluded from the academic community and could eventually attain professional privileges, they embodied the developing professional standards by which the discipline constructed its own identity. As we well know, however, present-day college entrance apparatuses and procedures are far more complex and multifaceted, involving college placement as well as college admission decisions, and are based upon a combination of indicators elicited by nationally standardized tests in addition to examinations administered by individual institutions.

In this book I have chosen to confine my analysis of current entrance examinations in English to the verbal portion of the Scholastic Aptitude Test (SAT). I do this because although I realize that the verbal SAT is by no means the only instrument used to define literacy as a college entry-level requirement, I am also aware of the overwhelming tendency on the part of those concerned about the nation's literacy education to draw conclusions about the condition of academic literacy and the quality of literacy education from the single measure of verbal SAT scores.

As my study reveals, there are also historical and institutional reasons that justify the selection of the verbal SAT as the single most significant descendent of the earliest college entrance examinations in English. The initial impulse toward standardizing entrance requirements—an impulse that eventually culminated in the establishment of the College Board and its more widely known administrative agency, the Educational Testing Service (ETS)—came from the collective energies of individual departments of English. At the heart of the standardization movement was a concern for the academic institutionalization of vernacular literacy in the wake of the demise of the language-based classical curriculum. The pages that follow tell a story of the academy's appropriation of vernacular literacy through the development of English studies as a separate area of academic specialization and of English studies' eventual surrender, to external assessment agencies, of direct responsibility for defining literacy as "the center of the educational enterprise."

I conclude with a call for the reestablishment of literacy as the unifying concern of English studies. In taking such a position, I am aware of the good company I keep. Most assuring is the presence of educational critics Jay Robinson, Myron Tuman, Raymond Williams, and others. It is my hope for this book that its historical perspective and its specific focus on the development of institutional structures for literacy testing at the college entry level will contribute additional depth and richness to their descriptions of the institutional identity of English studies. Finally, I hope that my study may provide a basis for discussions about productive directions for the future growth of the English studies profession.

Acknowledgments

I would like to acknowledge with gratitude the University of Iowa's summer support that provided me with the material means to finish this book. Equally if not more important are the inspiration and assistance of various individuals throughout the writing process. Foremost among them are Stephen Witte, Keith Walters, Beth Daniell, and Lester Faigley, intellectual companions during my early interest in literacy and assessment. Thanks are likewise due to James Berlin, who early on suggested to me that history might be even more interesting than I imagined. Thanks, too, to my manuscript reviewers, Deborah Brandt and Kathryn Flannery, and to my sisters, JoAnn Campbell and Elizabeth Hodges, for their unflagging interest in me and my work. And finally, for their support and goodwill, I am grateful to my colleagues in the University of Iowa's rhetoric department: Fred, Bonnie, Barbara, Ralph, Gene, Deb, Cleo, Margaret, Dennis, Don, Takis, Carol, Cyndi, Doug, and Allison.

In an even deeper realm of gratitude, I thank my children, Karlina, John, and Julian, for their support on the home front and my husband, Ben, for his cheerful willingness to assume the roles of computer technician, coequal caregiver, and then some.

Institutionalizing Literacy

CHAPTER ONE

Formal and Functional Definitions of Literacy

Two theoretical currents that animate discussions of literacy today are those that emphasize *formal* aspects of written text and those that focus on ways that written text *functions* to mediate human social interactions. In attempting to describe this theoretical dichotomy, Keith Walters, Beth Daniell, and I several years ago identified contradictory assumptions that we believed to be underlying the two theories as they describe opposite ends of the literacy research spectrum. Central to a formalist perspective, we argued, is a concern with the mastery of forms of cognition as well as mastery of certain textual forms a writer may choose for translating thought into language. Representing that school of thought is an impressive and influential body of research constructed by such scholars as Eric Havelock, Jack Goody and Ian Watt, Walter Ong, and David Olson. The thrust of their research supports the proposition that acquiring literacy causes fundamental changes in human cognition on both an individual and a cultural level. Opposing that camp are "functionalists" such as Freire, Heath, Brandt, and Aronowitz and Giroux, who are concerned with ways that readers and writers use written text to interact with one another to accomplish social and material goals.

I will briefly present the essential arguments constructing both these descriptions of literacy in order to prepare the ground for a subsequent discussion of the differing approaches to literacy instruction that they have been called upon to support. In the course of this discussion it becomes apparent that formalist assumptions have developed in large part from a desire to trace the heritage of a particularly influential type of discourse—that is, academic discourse—whereas functionalist assumptions derive from pedagogical concerns that have arisen primarily outside academic contexts. To be sure, functional- based approaches to literacy instruction have been implemented with varying degrees of success and failure in academic settings, but as I argue in this book, their influence has been considerably limited by their incompatibility with academically acceptable methods of literacy assessment. It is, after all, much easier to describe the dimensions of language forms than it is to capture the dynamic and contextually dependent process of functioning communication.

Because of the importance of assessment within the institutional structure of the American educational system from the early grades on through advanced levels of higher education, measurability becomes profoundly significant in determining how the academy will conceptualize its various subject areas and their methods of instruction. Judith Langer's 1984 study of the role of testing in classroom teaching suggests that the evaluative function of education often, in fact, usurps the instructional, nonevaluative function. Langer summarizes her findings by noting that "what seems to be happening in the classrooms . . . is that the *instructional* phase of the model has virtually disappeared, being replaced by an incessant cycle of practice and testing" (114).

In English studies—the academic discipline that most directly serves as the custodian of literacy and the arbiter of the academy's literacy standards—the function of assessment, whether for descriptive or evaluative purposes, is especially important, since reading and writing are so central to our concept of education. For all intents and purposes, a "literacy crisis" is synonymous with a "crisis in education" because literacy is the privileged medium of information exchange in virtually all academic subject areas. In describing the complex interrelationship between literacy and schooling in our society, Galtung maintains that literacy serves as a "launching pad" for further schooling (271); the ability to read and write, he explains, constitutes "the first rung on the ladder (or succession of ladders) of schooling" (277). Observing that the content of Western schooling is primarily verbal, Galtung goes on to explain that "knowing how to read and write is a *conditio sine qua non* for participation" in the educational system that is recognized and respected by our culture (277). Stein makes a similar point when she analyzes the special concern critics of education have directed toward the schools' programs for teaching reading and writing:

> "The development of verbal literacy" has loomed as an ominous problem because the success of instructional pro-

grams in the sciences is thought to depend directly on the knowledge and skills acquired in learning how to read and write. For that matter, the development of reading skill is believed to be central to almost every aspect of intellectual pursuit in the American schools. (1)

Because literacy as an academic skill occupies this uniquely "facilitating" position among all branches of academically fostered knowledge and ability, the terms *literacy* and *education* are often used interchangeably, and this time-honored identification between literacy and education lies near the heart of what I will be calling "formal" definitions of literacy—definitions that assume a history of literacy in which formal features of texts directly represent aspects of literate cognition.

Formal Definitions of Literacy

An identification between literacy and formal education finds its roots in antiquity, when philosophers and Sophists alike objectified language in order to describe its function as a vehicle for truth seeking or persuasion. As we will see, the capacity for language to objectify thought and, in turn, the capacity for written text to objectify language chart a history of academic progress that informs the formalist school of literacy theory and is celebrated in that theory. Literate cognition and culture, for theorists in this camp, are epitomized by academic modes of thought, and stages in the development of these modes have been captured and recorded in an evolutionary progression of textual forms.

The narrative running through formalist scholarship is a narrative of separation and exclusion. Literate culture is described according to its distinctness from oral culture where human memory rather than written text preserves cultural norms and truths. Formalists such as Havelock, Goody and Watt, Ong, and Olson observe that by taking over the function of memory, alphabetic literacy "restructures consciousness," freeing portions of the intellect to function in the distinctly literate mode of formal-analytic thought. Literacy thus implies a separation for individuals—and, by extension, for cultures—from an oral past in which human interaction was essential for communication and cultural continuity.

The separation occurs by virtue of literacy's power of objectification. Literacy enables us to transform the evanescence of speech—and the even greater intangibility of thought—into a textual artifact. Thus embodied in written text, which can be transported through time and space, thought and language are freed from the constraints of any particular social context. The individuals who can inscribe their thoughts in writing are no longer dependent on another human presence to help them create transferable meaning. Like memory, the attention they would otherwise have to devote to monitoring the expenditure of conversational resources between themselves and others can be focused more uninterruptedly upon the symbolic construction of meaning, with alphabetic symbols serving as the basic building blocks.

I do not wish to imply that formal literacy theorists exclude the social or interactive function of written language altogether, but they are less interested in the conversational or affective aspects of written communication than in the way that writing manifests in symbolic form an extension of human cognition. They are chiefly interested in what Vygotsky would term the "symbolizing" component of human nature, and they look to written text as an observable record of this particular variety of human activity. Theirs is a concern with how text interposes itself between writers and readers, functioning in effect to shield rhetor and audience from each other's intellectually distracting social demands.

Undeniably, literacy does enable communication to escape the here and now of a specific social context in a way that orality does not. A text written in twelfth-century France can be read, understood, and, in a sense, responded to in twentieth-century America. Formal literacy theory is less concerned, however, with text's capacity to forge interpersonal connections across expanses of time and space than with its isolating capacities. Written text enables writers to be alone with their thoughts and intentions; it facilitates, in other words, the paradoxical development of a solitary communicator.

The interactions that formal literacy theory privileges, then, are not those that occur between writers and readers, but those that occur, symbolically, between writers or readers on the one hand and texts on the other. Such human-object interactions, according to formalists, promote the development of rational, objective ways of thinking. Because they can be read and reread, written texts lend themselves to critical scrutiny; their propositions may be isolated from the flow of language, tested and challenged. In the central narrative of formal theory, this potential of literacy to extend rational thought has paved the way to a distinctly academic mode of knowledge construction. Such a connection is implicit in the ground-breaking work of Jack Goody who, upon observing that literacy was responsible for promoting an "increase in scope of critical activity, and hence of rationality, skepticism, and logic," proposes to "link the discussion [of literacy] to the history of scientific endeavor" (37). The theme of separation thus takes on additional significance as the history of literacy begins to account for a set of specialized language uses that serve to distinguish an educated, intellectual class from the culture at large. It is important to note that in the formalist discussion of literacy, the development and accomplishments of this academic subculture are granted the right to represent the overall culture's greatest developmental potential.

This is the theme that runs through much of Walter Ong's writing, as he locates the development of literacy in the history of the academy. When he writes of the potential of literacy to restructure consciousness, he is in fact concerned with how literacy has functioned to structure an exclusively *academic* consciousness that is reflected in the development of academic discourse. Ong's interest in confining the history of literacy specifically to the history of the academy is apparent in the importance he ascribes to "Learned Latin," meaning the Latin that served as the common language of Western scholarship from the Middle Ages until the nineteenth century but that had long before ceased to function as a vernacular. An exclusively masculine medium of communication, this variety of literacy incorporated a form and content that set the academy apart as an enterprise psychologically distanced from "the immediate interpersonal lifeworld where the word unites one human being with another" (*Interfaces* 25). Ong goes on to explain that the purposes for which Learned Latin were used were also markedly separate from those met by vernacular discourse in the world outside the academy and the professions it served. While various mother tongues functioned concretely as social currency among family and friends and in the marketplace,

Learned Latin was consistently used for "more or less abstract, academic, philosophical, scientific subjects or for forensic or legal or administrative or liturgical matters" (*Interfaces* 25).

It is important to note that Ong's discussion of the cognitive consequences of academic literacy, from Learned Latin to its present vernacular forms, is not value free. While acknowledging that academic literacy has been inaccessible to large portions of the population throughout the history of civilization—particularly, in Ong's account, to women—he identifies its very exclusivity as a necessary cause of intellectual progress. By facilitating an objective, rational stance, the written language of Learned Latin brought about the removal of the thinker-writer from the emotionally interruptive quagmire of what we might call "the real world" to a more "exquisite" realm of objective truth:

> Learned Latin effects even greater objectivity by establishing knowledge in a medium insulated from the emotion-charged depths of one's mother tongue, thus reducing interference from the human lifeworld and making possible the exquisitely abstract world of medieval scholasticism and of the new mathematical modern science which followed on the scholastic experience. Without Learned Latin, it appears that modern science would have got underway with greater difficulty, if it had gotten underway at all. Modern science grew in Latin soil, for philosophers and scientists through the time of Sir Isaac Newton commonly both wrote and did their abstract thinking in Latin. (*Orality* 114)

David Olson picks up the same theme in his examination of the "literate bias" in academic discourse. He too tells a tale of social separateness as he describes the development of essayist literacy, a distinctly academic brand of literacy that results from mastering the "'schooled' language of written texts" ("Utterance" 258). Building upon the work of such scholars as Havelock (1963), Parry (1971), Goody and Watt (1963), and McLuhan (1964), Olson argues that formal education in our culture imparts a brand of literacy in which meaning is located in the text rather than in an interaction of speakers based on shared intentions and understandings. Schooled literacy, in other words, assumes its ideal form in the currency of "explicit, autonomous statements." These statements are unambiguously expressed, and their truth status is dependent upon their being logically consistent with other claims and statements presented in the text rather than upon their correspondence with the real-life experience of the reader or the writer. The ideal text in the tradition of essayist literacy, then, is more importantly referenced to itself than to a socially constructed reality.

Like Ong, Olson traces the bias of formal logic as a structuring mechanism for written text to the ancient Greeks' invention of alphabetic script, an invention that led to a "literate revolution" in Western civilization. Like others in the formalist camp, Olson identifies as a consequence of this invention the development of an analytic, logical mode of thinking, made possible by the capacity of the written text to function as information storage, or memory. He supports his claim that alphabetic literacy is causally connected with this new way of perceiving the world by observing that in their transformation from an oral to a literate culture, the Greeks began to develop an elevated regard for prose as a medium for conveying knowledge. Freed from the need for certain prosodic features that served as mnemonic devices in poetry, prose came to be valued for the explicitness with which it could encode meaning. This characteristic stood in direct opposition to the ambiguity of poetry and oral language that allowed for—even invited—multiple interpretations. Prose, unlike poetry, could "speak for itself" independent of its author's intent. As Olson notes, "Prose statements were neither subtle nor devious; they tended to mean what they said" ("Utterance" 267).

Like Ong, Olson is concerned with written prose as it has become central to the academic undertaking of knowledge construction according to formalized rules of inquiry. Unlike speech, he maintains, writing was permanent enough to permit critical scrutiny that could lead to the detection of logical inconsistencies in the text. The resulting need for internal consistency in the production of written text led, in turn, to the formulation of rules of logic that if adhered to by a writer allowed a text to become autonomous.

Olson goes on to observe that the Greeks believed the system of formal logic provided rules for arriving at objective truth. With a contemporary understanding of the interdependence of thought and language, however, he corrects the ancients' perception by observing that what the Greeks understood as rules governing thought are more accurately described as rules governing language use. This complex relationship between thought and language, as we will see, is one that has complicated literacy testing throughout its history in the academy. While the examinations we will be looking at are often explicit about an academic community's concern with measuring students' mastery of rules governing the use of standard written English or production and interpretation of certain privileged genres of written text, adherence to these rules has often been taken as a measure of "intellectual power."

Whether described as rules of thought or as rules of language use, the Greeks' system of logic consisted of such operations as classification, analysis, definition, and comparison—operations that have figured prominently in the development of academic disciplines through the ages. As Myron Tuman has recently observed, these logical operations, by effecting a separation of subject and object, marked the emergence of a critical objectivity that is the hallmark of Greek and Western thought as they have been preserved in the academy. This distancing, objectifying impulse of literacy, according to Tuman, eventually "transforms the world" by making possible the evolution of specialized academic knowledge:

> No longer is verbal knowledge embodied in social relations; now, for the first time in human history, knowledge can be codified and stored in autonomous academic disciplines, independent of the beliefs of the population at large. The study of the past thus becomes formalized as history; the study of religion, theology; the study of public speaking, rhetoric; and the study of thinking, philosophy. In creating distinct areas of study, phonetic literacy also creates a new class of intellectuals, people who specialize in one or more areas of knowledge not widely shared by the group as a whole—a separation, Goody and Watt wryly point out, that leads to the ongoing tradition of jokes about absent-minded professors, the implication being that those who are better at what the group cannot do must somehow be

worse in what the group ordinarily does as a matter of course. (*Preface* 71)

Functionalist Definitions

In chapter 2, I will return to Tuman's privileging of specialized knowledge not widely shared by the group and examine it in light of the professionalization process that has been influential in structuring the modern American academy. I am particularly concerned, of course, with the professionalization process as it has affected the development of English studies, since the professional values of that discipline are those most readily summoned when the need arises for literacy standards to be articulated as public policy. Before I turn my attention to the fit between formalist definitions of literacy and institutional implementations of literacy testing, however, I want to briefly explore some of the central tenets of functionalist definitions of literacy. Although these tenets have developed largely outside the academic context, they have not been entirely absent from the academic scene. In fact, as subsequent chapters will demonstrate, arguments that literacy should be functionally based have periodically surfaced in debates surrounding the purposes of American education and the testing methods that could best enforce educational goals. The presence of functional notions about literacy has been particularly apparent during times when student populations have undergone sudden growth and transformation. At such times functional definitions have tended to coincide with arguments for greater democratization of education and the establishment of academic standards that acknowledge the strengths of students from a diversity of backgrounds.

But first, some clarification of the term *functional literacy,* since I do not intend it to signify "minimum competence," the meaning that functional literacy often acquires in educational settings. Typically, *minimum competence* is understood as an individual's ability to "get by" in a literate society—to function, but just barely. According to these standards, individuals who are functionally literate may be able to fill out job applications, sign checks, read road signs and labels on consumer goods, and respond to want ads in the classified section of a newspaper, but they are unlikely to be able to use literacy to engage in critical reflection or to effect personal or social change. Absent from such an understanding of literacy are the notions of individual empowerment and social progress that are so dear to American beliefs about the value of education and that exert such strong appeal in the writings of formal literacy theorists.

The tendency to associate functional literacy with minimal survival skills results, no doubt, from the nonacademic origins of the concept. The term *functional literacy* first appeared during World War II when the United States Army needed to sort servicemen according to their abilities to understand written instructions for performing military tasks. In the decade following the war, the term became increasingly important as well in UNESCO's attempts to define the goals of literacy education in underdeveloped countries, and it is with such a population of learners—the poor, the unemployed, the culturally alienated—that the term continues to be linked. These nonacademic origins, I believe, hold special significance for the development of an alternative to the formalist perspective on literacy. Nevertheless, I reject the implication of minimal competence and instead present a much expanded definition of functional literacy, one deriving in part from the philosophy behind Paulo Freire's pedagogy and incorporating an understanding of literacy as a critical and a materially functional ability.

While the formalist construction of literacy celebrates the heritage of academic language use, functionalists are typically concerned with the use of written language for something other than "doing school." Most prominently implemented in settings and among populations far from the mainstream educational community, functional literacy programs focus on the learners' perceived literacy needs while rejecting the school-imposed system of grade-level equivalencies as a measure of progress in literacy learning. Karl Haigler, former head of the Adult Literacy Initiative at the United States Department of Education and currently head of Mississippi's Literacy Initiative, for instance, opposes his brand of literacy instruction to the credentialing process of school instruction, though many of his goals are in line with the stated goals of many academic institutions. In a recent interview for *The Atlantic* Haigler explained:

> We're getting rid of the "grade-level" thinking that says a person is literate when he or she obtains a high-school-equivalency diploma. Literacy is better defined as a contin-

uum of skills, ranging from simple decoding of written matter to high levels of critical thinking and problem-solving. Programs need to be redesigned to meet a whole array of actual social needs, from the assembly-line worker who needs to read charts and manuals to the person whose greatest desire is to read her Bible. (qtd. in Maslow 31–32)

Developers of the Mississippi Literacy Initiative, which has gained positive national prominence for the state, reject the traditional methods of "teaching adults to read—in a vacuum, without taking into account their own immediate hopes and aims—"(Julie Mabus, qtd. in Maslow 31) and turn instead to precedents set by the radical educator Paulo Freire in Brazil and Nicaragua. Freire's writings on the pedagogy of the oppressed are perhaps the most thorough articulation of functional literacy theory available today. In *The Pedagogy of the Oppressed*, Freire outlines the rationale behind his approach, which is deeply rooted in the belief that literacy, like education in general, is a social practice through which power relationships are enacted. Like the formalists, he is concerned with history, but it is a history of quite a different character. Whereas the formalists tell of the intellectual accomplishments of their academic ancestors, Freire tells the history of oppression at the hands of those same ancestors who have held a monopoly on literacy, education, and other means of access to privilege and power.

As a group, functionalists present a historical account of literacy that is embedded in a continuing succession of social and political contexts, and they fault the formalists' version of history for attempting to isolate a single, privileged strand of cultural development from its social underpinnings. Thus, American exponents of functional theory, Stanley Aronowitz and Henry Giroux, reject the educational reforms advocated by such contemporary formalists as E. D. Hirsch and Allan Bloom on the basis of their distortion of cultural history to impose "a view of culture removed from the trappings of power, conflict, and struggle." The outcome of establishing such a version of cultural history, according to Aronowitz and Giroux, is "to legitimate a view of learning and literacy that not only marginalizes the voices, languages, and cultures of subordinate groups but also degrades teaching and learning to the practice of implementation and mastery" ("Schooling" 183).

Aronowitz and Giroux seek to replace the formalists' "pedagogy of transmission"—that is, a transmision of cultural artifacts preserved in revered written texts and standardized forms of written language—with a dialogic pedagogy that promotes the use of literacy to engage students and teachers in critical examination of history and culture. Once again, Freire is a key figure in promoting the brand of critically functioning literacy that Aronowitz, Giroux, and other leftist educational reformers prescribe for American curricula and classrooms.

In Freire's pedagogical scheme, the social situation constructed by students and teachers together provides the shape and direction of what Freire terms "authentic education." The model for this sort of education is that of a dialogue in which hierarchical divisions are broken down so that teachers become teacher-learners, and learners become learner-teachers. Educational values are thus determined not by a mandate to perpetuate an established academic tradition but by local conditions and by the emerging purposes and realizations of educators and learners in social interaction with one another. This socially situated version of education stands in opposition to the "banking concept" of traditionally conceived schooling. Describing the shortcomings of the latter approach, Freire claims that "many political and educational plans have failed because their authors designed them according to their own personal views of reality, never once taking into account (except as mere objects of their action) the *men-in-a-situation* to whom their program was ostensibly directed" (83).

In accordance with these nonacademic origins, attempts to import functional literacy into an academic setting often emphasize ways literacy is used in the family and community life of students who are academically marginalized. The ethnographic work of Shirley Brice Heath in this country represents an effort to describe the poor fit between the social functions of literacy in such students' home communities and the educational ideals of schooled literacy. Heath concludes from her study of a small Piedmont community, which she calls Trackton, that the functions and consequences of literacy in any society are dependent upon the literacy requirements of an individual community's cultural ideology as well as material factors such as the availability of writing equipment and reading materials and the constraints of time and energy demands.

Unlike the formalists, who see in the literacy accomplishments of the academic community the realization of literacy's greatest potential, Heath offers a pragmatic argument, suggesting that academic essayist literacy does not serve the real-life needs of its students. She hypothesizes that within the bureaucratic culture of the United States the functions of literacy among the general population may be more in harmony with those of Trackton, South Carolina, than with the school system's representation of literacy:

> Understanding and responding to the myriads of applications, reporting forms, and accounting brochures which daily affect the lives of nearly every family in the U.S. bears little resemblance to the decoding of extended prose passages or production of expository writing, the two literacy achievements most associated with school success. ("Functions and Uses" 133)

Heath's concern that the academic community with its espousal of formal literacy is too far removed from real-life concerns, and especially those of students who are unsuccessful in school, is a theme she shares with Deborah Brandt, who advocates an "involvement focused" definition of literacy as a *social* rather than an isolating activity. Brandt argues that such a definition, which she contrasts with a formalist "text-focused" definition, ultimately compels a "reanalysis of literacy failures in school" (7). She suggests that the academic community should reconceive literacy as a social interaction between writer and reader and that the requisite knowledge for literacy learners must therefore be the ability to maintain social contact with the reader or writer of the text. This, according to Brandt, is more essential to the successful practice of literacy than is the mastery of textual forms that facilitate the creation of an autonomous text. In fact, Brandt maintains, texts never really can be autonomous; they only come to life when they mediate a social interaction between reader and writer.

The Formal-Functional Opposition and the Inclusive-Exclusive Paradox of Language

An obvious point of difference between Brandt's definition and a formalist understanding of literacy is the degree of social involvement assumed by each approach. As Brandt has pointed out, the strand of literacy theory that I have identified as formalist (and that she refers to as "strong-text" literacy theory) is antisocial in its fundamental assumptions. Attributing primary importance to oral-literate contrasts, theorists of that school concentrate on describing not only how literacy differs from orality but also on how it makes literate people different from those who are illiterate. Literacy, according to their definition, gains its primary importance as a code of exclusion, even as it provides a means of mutual recognition among members of the academic community.

At this point it is important to remember that literacy, a subcode of language, itself entails a variety of sub-subcodes, as Scribner and Cole reveal in their studies of the three types of literacy practiced by the Vai of Liberia. Heath makes a similar point in her comparative studies of the forms and functions of literacy in three neighboring communities in the Piedmont. While Heath's subjects from both the black and the white working-class communities certainly possess literacy skills and apply them to a variety of ends, neither of the communities privileges the school-oriented literate and preliterate activities dominant in the nearby white middle-class homes. On the basis of this realization, Heath faults a monolithic academic understanding of literacy for the difficulties the working-class children in her study experience in learning to read and write in school. She advocates instead a pluralistic notion of literacy, one in which the different communities within the domain of a single national culture are viewed as analogous in their diversity to the multinational communities served by UNESCO. What the working-class children and their teachers must engage in, then, is a process of *translating* among the disparate codes of literacy at home and at school so that teachers and students become mutually understandable. Similarly, Freire's concept of dialogic pedagogy is intended to accomplish a sort of translating between divergent perspectives. Dialogue, in Freire's system, really means shared responsibility for "naming" the world. It is the development of a common language or naming system that breaks apart the I-Thou dichotomy and enables individuals to engage in purposeful communication with one another. As Freire explains:

> In the dialogical theory of action, Subjects meet in cooperation in order to transform the world. The antidialogical,

dominating *I* transforms the dominated, conquered *thou* into a mere *it*. The dialogical *I*, however, knows that it is precisely the *thou* ("not-I") which has called forth his own existence. He also knows that the *thou* which calls forth his own existence in turn constitutes an *I* which has in his *I* its *thou*. The *I* and the *thou* thus become, in the dialectic of these relationships, two *thous* which become two *I's*. (167)

It seems then that any attempt to take into account the distance between formal and functional definitions of literacy must derive from a theory of language that is consistent with the process of translation. In attempting to formulate such a theory we can turn to the work of George Steiner, who argues that while language universally functions for the ostensible purpose of communicating—of uniting human beings through shared consciousness—it also serves, at the same time, the paradoxical function of preserving the privacy of the linguistic community and even, in the case of idiolects, of the individual. Translation, according to his scheme, is often necessary *within* languages as well as *between* them, even though the need may be obscured by apparent linguistic commonality. It is easy to see why translation must operate to enable, say, a Russian speaker or writer to communicate with an American; it is less obvious that the variety of dialects and grapholects that together constitute American English must also undergo a sort of translation process to be mutually understandable. Steiner illustrates this phenomenon of linguistic exclusivity with reference to "special languages" that protect the integrity of small, select groups within the larger community and then describes how similar patterns of selection and exclusion operate in the dialects of social and ethnic subcultures:

> Different castes, different strata of society use a different idiom. Eighteenth-century Mongolia provides a famous case. The religious language was Tibetan; the language of government was Manchu; merchants spoke Chinese; classical Mongol was the literary idiom; and the vernacular was the Khalka dialect of Mongol. In very many cases, such as the sacred speech of the Zuni Indians, such differences have been rigorously formalized. Priests and initiates use a vocabulary and formulaic repertoire distinct from everyday language. But special languages—hieratic, masonic, Ubuesque, mandarin, the semi-occult speech of the regimental

mess or fraternity initiation—pose no essential difficulty. The need for translation is self-evident. Far more important and diffuse are the uses of inflection, grammatical structure, and word choice by different social classes and ethnic groups to affirm their respective identities and affront one another. It may be that the agonistic functions of speech inside an economically and socially divided community outweigh the functions of genuine communication. . . . languages conceal and internalize more, perhaps, than they convey outwardly. (31–32)

Steiner's observations about the exclusionary function of language and the consequent need for intralanguage translation provide a helpful scheme for examining the tensions between formal and functional approaches to defining literacy. The attention of formalists, it may be seen, is focused primarily upon the *exclusive* potential of literacy. They are especially concerned with discovering how literacy may have functioned historically to constitute and preserve the integrity of a particular subcommunity of literate individuals, namely the academic community whose heritage they themselves share. Formal literacy theory has been produced almost exclusively by individuals who conduct their theoretical explorations in an academic capacity and present them to an academic audience. Understandably, the perceptions and insights of these theorists are guided in large part by values derived from their own lived experience as academic literates. Not only have they learned to read and write in school environments, but their livelihood depends largely upon their continued success in an academic profession.

Functionalists, on the other hand, tend to define their position defensively against the academic status quo. In arguing for a process-oriented involvement-focused literacy theory, for instance, Deborah Brandt begins by dismantling the assumptions of what she describes as the "prevailing" strong-text theory that has provided "such an appealing model for school-based literacy" in the composition and reading classroom (104). Because they typically are reacting against what they perceive as an "ivory tower" concept of literacy, functionalists tend to be concerned with the process of "translating" across social boundaries such as those imposed by differences of class and ethnicity. In prescribing a pedagogy for the oppressed, Freire draws upon his "early sharing in the life of the poor" rather than on his academic credentials in formulating the essentially functional concept of critical literacy. It was this early exposure to poverty and subsequent "concrete situations" in the course of his educative activities with laborers and members of the middle class, he reports, not "thought and study alone," that sensitized him to the underclass "culture of silence" and enabled him to see the established educational system's agency in maintaining that culture in order to safeguard its own hegemony (21).

Richard Shaull, in his introduction to the English translation of *Pedagogy of the Oppressed,* singles out Freire's antagonism toward the established academic community as a key to significant parallels between Latin America's educational failures and our own. Regarding our own experience of being objectified and silenced by advanced technology, he writes: "The young perceive that their right to say their own word has been stolen from them, and that few things are more important than the struggle to win it back. And they also realize that the educational system today—from kindergarten to university—is their enemy" (15).

Obviously the "translation" that Shaull and Freire envision is not a one-way process in which an underclass of learners comes to master the dominant academic code. Rather, it is a dialogic process in which teachers and students together forge a new language.

Closer to home, we read the same antiacademic sentiment in composition research that villianizes the five-paragraph theme and the perceived dominant formalist pedagogy of which it is emblematic. Voices that express this view decry the importance that the mainstream pedagogy and testing paradigm attribute to formal correctness in terms of grammar, punctuation, syntactical structures of Standard Written English, and the privileging of established literary devices and genres. Functionalists argue that the value of form is secondary to that of function—that formal concerns such as those listed above are merely "surface-level" concerns while the true essence of literacy is captured by such considerations as communicative purpose, individual motivation, and the reader's or writer's positioning within a field of social forces that affect communicative possibilities.

Although a pedagogy focused on these "more fundamental" aspects of literacy may not point the way to academic success within the established educational system, functionalists argue, it can guide students toward the more skillful and effective use of literacy to accomplish social and material goals. The desired end of functional pedagogy is to enable learners to use literacy as a tool to "transact" the business of life—to penetrate more deeply into Ong's "interpersonal lifeworld" rather than to withdraw from it.

Such was certainly the thinking behind the Executive Committee of the College Composition and Communication Conference's historic endorsement of the "Student's Right to His Own Language" statement in 1972. This statement positioned the committee squarely in line with the functionalists by diminishing the importance of formal elements of Standard Written English while exalting the communicative capacity of language to express human "identity and style":

> We affirm the students' right to their own language—the dialect of their nurture in which they find their identity and style. Any claim that only one dialect is acceptable should be viewed as attempts of one social group to exert its dominance over another, not as either true or sound advice to speakers or writers, nor as moral advice to human beings. A nation which is proud of its diverse heritage and of its cultural and racial variety ought to preserve its heritage of dialects. We affirm strongly the need for teachers to have such training as will enable them to support this goal of diversity and this right of the student to his own language. (qtd. in Pixton 247)

It is significant that the CCCC Executive Committee here pledges its allegiance to a national identity, which can claim a "diverse heritage," rather than to an academic identity, which cannot. Implicit in the statement is the proposition that education serves the goals and values set by a broader public than the academic community. Literacy education, in other words, means something other than "doing school," and the responsibilty of teachers is to equip their students not merely for academic success, but for success in some broader notion of "life."

Predictably, in light of a popular and powerful tendency to view the academy as the arbiter of cultural and linguistic standards, the CCCC's statement has stirred more controversy than any other action undertaken by the organization. Objecting to the statement on the grounds that Standard English is essential for precise communication in an academic setting, William Pixton, for instance, has argued that dialects exist on a spectrum of intimacy and that dialect choice is influenced by the impression one wants to make on a particular audience. Standard Written English is the most general, or public, dialect on this spectrum, and an inability to command its specialized syntax and vocabulary severely limits a student's capacity for meaningful communication within the academic community. Pixton's position, which has much in common with the essentially formalist argument behind E. D. Hirsch's *Cultural Literacy*, is a defense of the academic status quo and rests upon a conviction that teachers' responsibility is to guide students to scholastic success, far removed from the entanglements of human intimacy to which the "lifeworld" outside the academy falls prey.

Toward an Understanding of How Formal and Functional Definitions of Literacy Have Shaped Debates over Academic Standards

I have concluded this chapter with a look at the controversy that has surrounded the "Student's Right to His Own Language" statement since its adoption by the CCCC in 1971, because the terms of the controversy have, throughout the past 100 years, structured an ongoing discussion about the purpose of education as represented in the academy's definition of literacy. In this debate, college entrance examinations in English have played a key role for two very important reasons. First is the "gatekeeper" function of entrance examinations. In a very literal sense, entrance exams have in the past and continue today to be instrumental in decisions made by members of the academic community as to who may join their ranks and who may not. In this regard we see the exams' accordance with the exclusionary potential of formal definitions of literacy. As chapter 2 will demonstrate, this exclusionary function has been supported by the development of a professional identity within English studies departments in the academy as well as by periodic increases in the student population that have brought about a practical need for greater selectivity among applicants to college.

College entrance examinations in English are especially important, too, for their articulatory function in bridging the gap between high school and college. As chapter 2 explains, the standardization movement that has so influenced entrance examinations was spearheaded by teachers and professors of English when the public and private educational systems in this country sought to merge—or at least to establish some continuity between themselves that would allow students to move from one system to the other. During the negotiations surrounding this merger, public high schools, which perceived their mission to be "education for life," engaged in strenuous debates with the private preparatory schools, which adhered to an ideology of "education for college." The opposing strands of this debate, as we read in the continuing controversy surrounding the "Student's Right" statement, continue to enliven discussions about the purpose of education today.

In the historical course of this ongoing discussion, American life has continued to undergo its own transformative changes as a result of developments in the U.S. economy, periodic waves of immigration, and America's changing status in international politics. Because in the final analysis the American academy necessarily remains a part of the broader American scene, such transformations are inevitably registered in the changing identity of the academy itself. As a consequence of history, then, "education for life" and "education for school" are both directed at moving targets whose courses may merge and separate through time in response to cultural ideologies and material conditions. The resulting difficulties of defining education's purpose in America raise questions—to be addressed in chapter 2—concerning the academy's dual role as a leader and shaper of society on the one hand and as a responder to societal demands on the other. By focusing on the historical development of entrance examinations in English, chapter 2 reveals how these dual functions of the American academy play out the familiar paradoxical themes of academic exclusivity and inclusiveness that weave through formal and functional definitions of literacy.

CHAPTER TWO

Academic Appropriation of Literacy and the Cult of Testing

In describing literacy as a practice whose historical evolution is the very backbone of human intellectual and cultural progress, formal literacy theorists effectively demonstrate how the academic community has "appropriated" literacy as its exclusive domain. As we have seen, formalist theory pays special attention to literacy's capacity for objectifying the union of thought and language in the external form of a cultural artifact. Because language is representational, such an artifact always functions to some extent as a historical record of external reality, but more importantly in the formalist scheme of things, it constitutes a symbolic representation of its writer's internal reality. Readers of written texts, in turn, have the opportunity to examine, criticize, and build upon writers' thought processes even in the absence of the writers themselves. By thus providing a symbol system through which the range of human cognitive activity may be extended, literacy constitutes a technology capable of directing as well as recording human culture.

To the extent that our society has designated schools as sites for both the preservation and production of culture, literacy itself becomes, as Jenny Cook-Gumperz terms it, the "essential product" of schools. A considerable body of research, however, testifies that it is by no means inevitable that literacy production should be the exclusive province of a formal educational system, nor has it always been so, even in our own cultural history. Soltow and Stevens, for example, trace the history of literacy education in America and observe that prior to the development of a modern, highly bureaucratized system of mass education, many people acquired literacy outside of academic contexts, in small, informal, localized groups. They claim, moreover, that the development of universal education in America was directed by a ruling-class desire to bring literacy under the control of a single, state-sponsored system of education. This desire was motivated by a fear that literacy's power to enact social transformation could be a dangerous weapon in the hands of members of the working class, were they not properly socialized to accept the authority of established social institutions. The wrong kind of literacy—or literacy used in the wrong way and for unapproved ends—might encourage workers to become dissatisfied with their lot in life and desirous of social and material advantages.

Once universal literacy did emerge as a national objective in the wake of the nation's industrialization, the potential danger of social disruption at the hands of the newly literate underclasses, according to Cook-Gumperz, was effectively mitigated by the schools' standardization of language in the form of "schooled literacy," described as "a system of decontextualized knowledge validated through test performance" (41). What distinguishes schooled or academic literacy from other possible varieties of literate activity—for instance, those validated by the Mississippi Literacy Initiative or Freire's critical literacy programs in Latin America—is a production process that is heavily dependent upon the mechanism of literacy testing.

The production of literacy through testing is of course legitimized by a modern consensus that education in general is a matter of progressing through successive levels of certification. This conception of education as a credentialing process derives, in turn, as Berlin's historical account of writing instruction in American colleges suggests, from events that led to the transformation of the old, elitist classical college into the modern university, which has presented itself as a meritocracy offering upward mobility through certification. But certainly this test-dominated version of education has not been without its detractors. Charges against American education's "cult of testing" are vehement and widespread, and Cook-Gumperz is by no means alone when she argues that instead of enforcing the impartial standards of an intellectual meritocracy, educational tests are more apt to function as mechanisms that enable an educated elite to impose exclusive standards upon academic aspirants. One such critic is Carolyn Marvin, who targets national standardized tests of literacy as instruments of social tyranny. Commenting that the culture of testing unites all school children in America, Marvin argues convincingly that standardized tests should be viewed as a form of mass communication that, like television advertising, assumes a silenced audience, submissive to the judgments of an anonymous, impersonal, and distant authority. In the case of such large-scale standardized literacy assessments, literacy's capacity to transcend the limitations of time and space and to reveal internal reality means little more than the extension via written text of a submissive relationship. Notions of "correct" or acceptable literate performance are thus revealed as products of "contests for social dominance." To acquire literacy in the American academic system, Marvin concludes, is to accept "increasing levels of regimentation" (78).

Critiques of literacy testing such as those offered by Marvin and Cook-Gumperz perform the valuable function of calling attention to testing as a medium of social construction. They point out that testing is not a socially neutral activity, but one that necessarily reflects the social predispositions of those who design, administer, and interpret tests. Even more important is the insistence of such critics that literacy testing be examined as a systematic enforcement of standards deriving from certain criteria of social rather than strictly intellectual inclusion and exclusion.

In these respects, both Cook-Gumperz and Marvin begin to take up Harvey Graff's challenge to study literacy in the institutional context of the American academy by responding to the "difficult but severe demand for critical examination of the *conceptualization of literacy* itself" ("Whither" 13). Joining forces with educational critics such as Michael Apple, Henry Giroux, and Stanley Aronowitz, they describe the growth of mass education as a process of centralizing authority, noting that within this process literacy tests have served as perhaps the primary means by which the dominant culture has constructed literacy as an educational product. In particular, they criticize increasingly standardized testing as the very means through which formal definitions of literacy are articulated, enforced, and legitimated. In requiring literacy to be measureable, tests assume that it is objectifiable, reducible to forms that can be isolated from the overwhelmingly complex variables of any given social context, and in requiring educational measurements to be standardizable, the interpreters of literacy tests impose the monolithic conceptualization of literacy that characterizes formal literacy theory.

Even though the use of literacy outside the schools is likely to be "tested" in functional terms, according to its communicative effectiveness, the schools' criteria for evaluating literacy are embodied in highly formalized examination settings. As a consequence, as Cook-Gumperz contends, school success characteristically depends less upon knowing how to use literacy than upon knowing how to demonstrate a mastery of certain standardized, formal features of literacy in artificial contexts designed by school authorities. Literacy is thus objectified as a "product" whose quality and quantity can be both measured and controlled by formal examinations.

Steiner's observation that language in any form works to define communities by simultaneously including members and excluding nonmembers, however, helps us to understand that academic literacy is more than simply a product of testing. It is, at the same time, the medium through which the academic community defines its own social boundaries and constitutes its membership. Academic literacy, in other words, is one of the academic community's primary means of establishing its separate, professional identity. Within this community, academic literacy does indeed function in ways that are presumably productive and meaningful to its users and that derive in part from a professional ethos that began to distinguish the academic community long before it assumed its modern form—prior to its endorsement of the vernacular as the privileged medium of knowledge production, organization, and transfer.

Cook-Gumperz astutely observes that it is because of its professional status that schooling has been able to establish a virtual monopoly on literacy as a standardized product. But as recent sociological studies of the professionalization process remind us, a professional product is a service, a form of labor that remains "inextricably bound to the person and the personality of the producer" (Larson 14). That is to say, the market value of professional products derives largely from the special, privileged status of their producers. The specialized training and socialization that professional producers receive become necessary attributes of those producers, functioning to distinguish their particular product or service for exchange on the professional market. In order for a profession to maintain market control, then, professional producers must themselves be produced.

What this means in terms of academic literacy is that literacy testing not only functions as a means of enforcing a product definition of literacy, but it must also be viewed as an avenue through which professional educators can establish a credentialed, professional identity. Literacy tests, and most conspicuously those controlling access to higher education where professional training takes place, thus become an important site for the ongoing market negotiations of professional educators. Professional identity, after all, must be carved out of a broader social milieu, from which a significant number of individuals assent to claims that certain types of expertise in the specialized construction of knowledge are indeed necessary and worthy of support. Accordingly, at the same time that literacy exams reflect the professional values of a far-reaching, state-endorsed educational system, they also reveal the formative influences of public demands for literacy as a professional product and for literacy "experts" who presumably can ensure the quality of its production and delivery.

While I am obviously much indebted to the critical insights of revisionists such as Cook-Gumperz, Marvin, Apple, and Giroux and Aronowitz, it is not my intention here to simply extend their vision, but rather to augment it with an internal analysis of the development of literacy tests in order to discover how they have served to construct the professional identity of English studies specialists, the academic tribe most closely involved with their formulation and use. The critics whose works are briefly considered above concern themselves chiefly with how academic literacy, increasingly represented by standardized tests, functions as a code of exclusion and a means of promoting literacy values, accomplishments and cultural attitudes of the dominant class achieved by identifying the failure of other groups to meet these standards. My own analysis of literacy tests, however, specifically those guarding the entrance to higher education, is guided by an equal desire to understand the internal dynamics of the standardization process, the struggles of a developing profession to define its commonality and its grounds of inclusion.

It is of course difficult, if not impossible, to discuss inclusion without also paying attention to exclusion, for as Steiner has shown in the case of linguistic codes, the two functions are but opposite sides of the same coin. In tracing the historical development of literacy tests at the college entrance level as a record of the professionalization of English studies, then, I am mindful of the extent to which professionalism is, always, a form of elitism that presupposes the necessary exclusion of "unqualified" individuals from access to its own professionally constructed knowledge base. To the extent that this knowledge is "arcane and scarce" and can therefore only be judged by those who possess it, exclusivity is the inevitable source of professional autonomy (Stricker, "Economic Success" 143). At the same time, I take seriously Larson's observation that the extent and direction of a professional product's standardization is profoundly influenced by the shared social characteristics of a group of professionals, for they are directly related to the group's criteria of inclusion as well as exclusion. As my historical account of the developing identity of English studies professionals demonstrates, however, it is important to realize that these "shared social characteristics" do not by any means describe a static entity. Indeed, the story of the professionalization of English studies that is recorded in and advanced by college entrance examinations in English reveals the "ruling class," itself, to be a construct in flux, shaped not only by its members' efforts to retain their hegemony but also by compromises and concessions to the demands of nonmembers seeking access to ruling-class privileges. Thus, as the history of college entrance examinations unfolds, we see that while American efforts to achieve universal literacy through the establishment of a widespread, coherent, and unified system of education may indeed be described as a process of centralizing authority through the monolithic construct of academic literacy, the very nature of that authority has changed dramatically over the course of time, and with it, accepted notions of academic literacy have changed as well.

Literacy Exams and the Development of English Studies Professionals: A Brief Overview

The final three decades of the nineteenth century were a transformative era in the history of American higher education. During this time the first American research universities were established in this country, beginning with Johns Hopkins in 1876 and followed thereafter by Clark University (1899), Stanford (1891), and the University of Chicago (1892). Modeled after the example of German universities, these institutions set the precedent of privileging graduate-level education and in so doing established an arena for the creation of highly specialized academic knowledge presided over by a new professional class of academic specialists. Concurrent with this development was the accelerating disintegration of the classical curriculum in American colleges, in part the result, as we shall see, of demands that grew out of the practical orientation of a fast- growing network of public schools.

The combined force of these two important developments near the end of the century provided an opportunity for the creation of a new professional group consisting of English language specialists and did much to ensure the success of their professionalization efforts. As "the language of the people," English embodied the pragmatic and democratic spirit of public education that was beginning to challenge the small group of private Eastern colleges and their attendant preparatory schools that, by the end of the nineteenth century, were nearly alone in championing the cause of classical literacy. In addition, English was hailed as the "new language of scientific learning" (Berlin, *Rhetoric and Reality* 22), and as such had acquired a considerable degree of respectability and power from its connection with the new and heavily funded research universities beginning to promote a culture of professionalism that was rapidly transforming middle-class occupations in the wake of the Industrial Revolution. Under circumstances such as these, and bolstered, moreover, by a language- and text-based academic heritage, members of the newly established departments of English were well positioned before the turn of the century to compete with their counterparts in the sciences for academic turf and professional status and prestige.

As participants in the transformation of the American academy, English studies specialists were building their professional identity during the competitive phase of American capitalism, an era described by Larson as primarily dependent upon the creation of new professional markets rather than upon the mere exploitation of existing markets for already recognized professional services. In describing the process by which such markets are created, Larson lists three essential steps, all of which, in the case of English studies, were served by the development of an increasingly standardized system of college entrance examinations. First among them is the careful definition of a particular body of specialized knowledge—to use Larson's term, a "cognitive basis" that the profession can claim as its exclusive domain. Secondly, in order to maintain exclusive control of this knowledge base and to ensure market stability, the profession must establish common standards of performance throughout its ranks. Professional services, in other words, like the cognitive basis from which they derive, must be standardized so as to be universally recognizable and distinct from similar services that might be offered by competing providers on the market. And finally, the profession must be able to reproduce itself by selectively recruiting new members and making sure that their development of professional expertise stays within the boundaries allowed by the specified knowledge base.

In meeting these three requirements for maintaining a professional identity based on cognitive exclusiveness, English studies professionals developed a credentialing process in which college entrance examinations have played a pivotal role. To be sure, a similar claim might be made for virtually all the modern academic professions. As Larson has noted, the primary means by which any profession acquires cognitive exclusiveness are credentialing requirements—among them "the license, qualifying exams, diplomas, and formal training in a common curriculum" (15). Similarly, Berlin, citing Bledstein, observes that in their quest for a "certifiable, professional designation," members of college English departments were simply participating in the same process as their colleagues in the sciences—a process in which the ability to control admission to the community was of utmost importance. "They too were struggling to define a specialized discipline, one akin to those of their counterparts in the new science departments in order to lay claim to the privilege and status accorded other new professions, and to serve as the certifying agency for admission to this select group" (*Rhetoric and Reality* 21).

In the specific case of English studies, however, the professional service being marketed—literacy instruction—plays such a central and facilitating position in the general schooling process that the setting of this professional group's admission standards, indirectly at least, influences access to nearly all the modern professions. At first glance this assertion may seem unfounded, since the literacy skills needed for acquiring the socialization and expertise demanded by other academically grounded professions such as civil engineering or nursing seem to have little connection with the theoretical knowledge that has come increasingly to describe the expertise of English studies specialists in the upper echelons of the profession. So far removed does this rarefied version of academic literacy seem to be from the concerns that structure our widespread perceptions of a literacy crisis in this country that an account of the professional development of English studies may seem irrelevant to any discussion of the academy's "essential product," literacy.

The history of English studies' professional development within the broader context of academic professionalization, however, places the matter in quite a different light. In spearheading the movement to standardize college entrance examinations at the end of the nineteenth century when American colleges were undergoing their transformation into the modern university system, the emerging departments of English studies played a key role in coordinating the processes of higher education and secondary schooling into an uninterrupted continuum, presumably grounded in "psychic principles" that governed the learning process from kindergarten through graduate levels of a university education. Most important to the development of their own identity, such educational coherence provided English studies professionals with the institutional structure necessary for gaining professional control of the "literacy market." It was only after the initially separate levels of elementary, secondary, and higher education were articulated into a single educational continuum that it became possible to conceptualize a single, standardized version of schooled literacy.

In large measure, the unification of American education was accomplished through the articulatory function of entrance exams that effected a consolidation of the originally unrelated systems of public and private schooling as well as secondary and higher education. For the newly emerging modern studies such as English in the nineteenth century, this consolidation at last enabled the production of professional knowledge, or theory, to occur at the same site as the production of professional practitioners, most importantly in the case of English studies, teachers. For this reason, it is significant that an offshoot of the academic legislation governing the development of standardized entrance examinations was the requirement that all secondary teachers should themselves have degrees from institutions of higher education. In 1899, when the National Education Association's Committee on College Entrance Requirements published its report containing the resolution that "teachers in the secondary schools should be college graduates, or have the equivalent of a college education" (30) the concept of higher education as a credentialing process was already beginning to take root, and the academic community was hard at work transforming education into a professional marketplace. The NEA committee, composed of six college professors and administrators and six secondary school teachers and administrators, explained the importance of professionally trained high school teachers thus:

> Our colleges and universities are now turning out each year numbers of young men and women of liberal training who are eager to teach subjects which they have been pursuing with enthusiastic devotion and distinguished success. Many of them have personal qualities which should fit them admirably for teaching. Surely, it is reasonable to urge that the best teachers for our high schools may be chosen from among them. Not only have they the requisite special knowledge, but they have given evidence that they possess the love of learning, lacking which the teacher is likely sooner or later to lose enthusiasm for his work and become a drudge.
>
> Fortunately, the policy of recruiting the high-school force from college graduates already prevails in many of our great cities, and there is little doubt that the practice will soon become general. It will react most happily on the higher education of our people by enlarging the field of work open to college men and women, and will be a potent influence in elevating our secondary schools to a position as dignified as that now held by the secondary schools of France and Germany. (30)

Classical Origins of English Studies

The effects of this professionalization process, facilitating as it did the exertion of a top-down influence by a group of academic specialists whose professional definition of their educational subject matter was privileged to be translated into public policy, were especially profound in the case of English studies, which until the nineteenth century was considered an unfit subject for academic study at the college level. During the first two centuries of American higher education, classical languages and classical texts comprised virtually all of the recognized college studies, the primary focus being grammar, rhetoric, and theological and philosophical disputations in the learned languages. It was not until 1745, when Yale became the first American college to require arithmetic as an entrance subject, that a college education began to mean something other than an education strictly in the classical languages. At the close of the eighteenth century and throughout the first half of the nineteenth, entrance requirements at the existing colleges registered the domination of classical languages by maintaining striking uniformity (see Nightingale; Broome), calling for the mastery of a small canon of Latin and Greek texts that varied only slightly from one college to the next. The only nonlanguage requirement for college admission during that time was a familiarity with the rules of vulgar arithmetic.

To fully appreciate the internal development of the professional structure and ideology of English studies, then, it is first helpful to know a bit about the American institutionalization of the classical curriculum from whose ashes English studies eventually arose. With the hastening collapse of classical studies throughout the nineteenth century, English language study emerged as the most direct heir of classical education's liberal tradition during a somewhat chaotic period of curricular reconstruction. Its firstborn status came not from its alignment with the modern scientific studies whose entry into the academy was truly revolutionary, but rather from its ability to conform to certain traditionally held, text-based educational ideals from which it gathered a certain amount of social respectability.

In their adherence to the classical languages, the early American colleges effectively constituted themselves as discourse communities set apart from the business of life in the world outside their walls. Students gained admission to these select communities by demonstrating their possession of a classical literacy through the command of formal rules of Greek and Latin grammar and through the ability to generate discourse in these languages. Just as the texts of classical authors served as the repository of academic knowledge, the classical languages, especially Latin, were the media through which members of the academic community were to exchange their thoughts and ideas. In keeping with these tenets, students during the seventeenth and eighteenth centuries were even forbidden to converse among themselves in the vernacular while on college property.

From the very beginning, higher education in America was closely identified with the creation and maintenance of a professional class of leaders. Initially that professional class was dominated by clergymen, who provided the nation's cultural leadership in moral and spiritual avenues. A recognition of the need for religious cultural leadership was, in fact, the single most important consideration in the founding of America's first colleges. Harvard, William and Mary, Yale, Brown, Princeton, and Columbia were all established as religious institutions of various Christian denominations and were intended to foster the sound moral and religious character of professional leaders in the New World. Their stated social mission was to supply the American people with an enlightened clergy, and indeed the majority of their graduates did go on to become clergymen. An early historian of American colleges, Cornelius Broome, calculated that of the 531 men who graduated from Harvard between 1638 and 1707, more than half entered the clergy. The ideal of religious cultural leadership was still very much in evidence even by the end of the nineteenth century. A survey of entrance requirements to the 422 American colleges and universities in existence in 1879, for instance, lists only 27 state universities and 48 nonsectarian institutions. The remaining 347 colleges and universities were affiliated with some denomination of Christianity (Nightingale).

Of lesser importance were the professions of medicine and law, which, although their most prestigious urban practitioners received their training in the colleges, were nevertheless served by a well-established apprentice system until well into the nineteenth century. And a large number of students at the pre–Civil War colleges were simply gentlemen's sons for whom college was a sort of finishing school where they prepared for the positions of aristocratic leadership that came with inherited property and wealth. In the latter capacity, American colleges carried on the tradition of the British universities where the social function of higher education was recognized and revered, and in an important sense this social value was also embodied in the separate code of classical literacy. Duffus traces the concept of a "gentleman's education" to the European Renaissance when the rich began to enter the universities. As the demographics of college student populations thus began to change, the significance of a knowledge of Latin, which had occupied the place of entrance examinations since the time of the medieval universities, began to change as well. During the Middle Ages, as Haskins records, the figure of the scholar was associated with poverty and monastic asceticism, and a command of Latin and Greek was an indication of the scholar's devotion to this scholastic ideal. During the Renaissance, however, literacy in the classical languages began to acquire social currency so that, as Duffus observes, "it was becoming fashionable to quote Greek and Latin tags" (13).

From such origins the American system inherited the concept of the educated gentleman who might go to college solely to become polished in speech and manner. In part, by virtue of their socialization in the language of the professions, educated gentlemen likewise participated in the privileges of professional status. While the real sorting mechanisms were more likely to be social connections and the ability to pay for a costly preparatory education, knowledge of the classical languages functioned as one of the primary means of distinguishing between an educated elect and the laboring masses. Latin and Greek came to embody what Steiner would term the "shared secrecy" of a group of language users that effectively functioned to exclude those who were not members. As Gerald Graff points out in his institutional history of literary studies in America, the professional ethic of early American colleges grew out of a tradition of liberal studies and was fundamentally opposed to the vocational values that we now associate with professional training. "College presidents spoke of 'gentle breeding' as a primary concern," Graff reports, "and saw the study of literature through the classics as a form of acculturation for 'the cultivated gentleman'" (20). These classically trained college men, as Edmund Wilson was later to observe, were expected to "preside over the arts and the professions" (qtd. in Graff 21) in fulfilling the destiny of cultural leadership for which they had been groomed.

Vernacular Academic Literacy and the Birth of English Studies

The institutionalization of modern subjects progressed gradually throughout the nineteenth century, during an era in the history of higher education that has been described as a time of "educational anarchy" (Duffus) and "chaotic diversity" (Farrand, "Brief History" 29), as each college and university struggled independently to formulate standards that would reflect its own educational ideals during the transitional period. The task was complicated by the interplay of various conflicting ideologies, manifested most conspicuously in confrontations between the then separate public and private school systems; between old, established eastern institutions and newly founded western schools; and between advocates of a scientific epistemology and staunch defenders of a liberal, humanistic approach to knowledge construction. In attempting to resolve these often bitter conflicts, the academic community focused its collective energies on college entrance requirements and their codification in the form of college entrance examinations. The gradual standardization of these devices across the country and throughout various types of institutions of higher education records a process of educational modernization following the fall of the classical curriculum. In this ongoing process, the academic community of English studies professionals has struggled to negotiate its position of cultural leadership, both by defining a professional expertise embodied in specialized forms and uses of language that distinguishes it from the culture at large and, at the same time, by asserting its professional responsiveness to public needs and demands. As an educational profession, English studies has sought to accomplish this twofold objective by attempting to integrate two conflicting ideologies: "education for life" and "education for higher education."

Vocationalism, Vernacular Literacy, and Public Secondary Education

The collapse of classical literacy's capacity to define an academic community signified, more than anything else, the failure of the community's patrician values to keep pace with political, economic, and social changes in the surrounding culture. Throughout the eighteenth and nineteenth centuries the practical value of classical languages in the traditional professions steadily waned, as scholarly texts became available in modern languages and as aristocratic notions about cultural leadership began to crumble before the forces of industrialization, vocationalism, and pragmatism that emerged under the protection of American democracy. Increasingly, the classical colleges and the preparatory schools serving them came under attack for their failure to address the real-life requirements and values of the American people. Perceiving these incompatibilities between the college culture and American life, President Francis Wayland of Brown University complained in 1842 that "in no other country is the whole plan for the instruction of the business of the young so entirely dissevered from connexion [*sic*] with the business of subsequent life" (qtd. in G. Graff 21).

A similar disenchantment with the impracticality of classical literacy in American colleges was even earlier evidenced by institutions of secondary education. During the Revolutionary era, the academy school system that sprang up in New England was intended as a practical alternative to an exclusively classical education. In addition to Latin and Greek, the academies undertook instruction in math and English in order to teach "the great end and real business of living" (Duffus 25) not addressed by the traditional preparatory curriculum. In light of this founding intent to educate for life rather than strictly for college, there is a certain irony in the fate of many of the more prominent academies, among them Phillips Exeter (1778) and Phillips Andover (1783), which were eventually absorbed by the college system to become preparatory schools during the rise of public secondary education in the nineteenth century.

A somewhat more successful attempt to undermine the stronghold of classical literacy was the founding of the Boston English High School in 1821. Espousing the ideal of education for life, it was intended as a terminal alternative to preparatory education. Neither Latin nor Greek was listed among its entrance requirements, and the classical languages did not appear anywhere on the school's outline of courses.

Throughout the nineteenth century the pragmatic approach to secondary education spread rapidly across the country as a growing system of public high schools offered educational opportunities beyond the common school to increasing numbers of students intent on futures that did not include college attendance. During those early years of American public secondary schooling, college preparation was by and large considered the province of the private preparatory schools that orbited the private, endowed colleges situated primarily in the New England and Middle Atlantic states. So separate did the public and private educational systems remain during much of the nineteenth century, in fact, that the public high school was often referred to as "the people's college"—the implication of course being that a high school diploma was a terminal degree. Students who attended public high schools were assumed to be destined for futures quite different from those of individuals whose formal education extended through preparatory school directly into college. The aims of the two educational systems were considered to complement but not intersect each other; while the colleges and universities were to prepare cultural leaders and policy makers, the public schools were to train men and women to be efficient workers under those leaders.

In no uncertain terms the essential difference between public and private education was one of class more than level of educational attainment. By the end of the nineteenth century, when a well-established system of state universities put higher education within easy reach of public high school graduates, the alleged superiority of a private school education derived from its exclusive claims to true, scholarly cultural production via classical literacy. In an 1891 article entitled "The Limitations of State Universities," Horace Davis blamed the pragmatic, utilitarian thrust of public education for advancing scientific rather than literary values, resulting in an educational product marked by "visible utility" rather than "brilliant scholarship" (437). More specifically, the public universities' inferiority stemmed from their mandate to extend the broad educational aims of the public secondary system, an end achieved by an accreditation admissions system. According to Davis, this system of admitting all students who had successfully completed the secondary course of study in a state-accredited high school necessitated a lowering of college standards and a loss of professional autonomy for higher education. Accreditation, he complained, "compels the university to keep its curriculum within reach of the school, and to maintain such entrance requirements as will be deemed useful studies by the Board of Education" (434). This same demand for "broad education," moreover, obliged the public universities to spread their available funds thinly, so that the traditionally revered mode of education in letters was forced to share resources with technical instruction, pedagogy, and "practical sciences" such as agriculture and mining. In short, Davis complained, public universities were forced to neglect classical training, without which men are not "finished scholars" (434).

More than twenty years later, Wilson Farrand, headmaster at the Newark Academy in New Jersey and a leading light in the initial push to standardize college entrance requirements, continued to maintain that private colleges were duty bound to uphold standards that could combat the spread of utilitarianism that nourished public education. "The primary purpose of the public school is to prepare the masses of our people directly and as quickly as possible, for efficient service and for citizenship," he wrote. "The chief object of college is to train men and women for leadership in the higher walks of life" ("Public School" 505).

It is interesting to note that Farrand's comments appeared at a time when English studies had gained a secure foothold in the college curriculum. By 1915, although vernacular literacy was firmly established as a practical replacement for classical literacy, the spirit of classical education, along with the traditional aristocratic and academic values that had been attached to classical literacy, survived the process of modernization and, as we shall see, lent its support to early efforts at defining the academic terrain of English studies. This was particularly true at the old, established eastern schools where the classical tradition was so firmly entrenched. In the western states, on the other hand, where establishments of higher education—primarily state-supported—did not appear until the nineteenth century when the classical tradition was already well into its decline, a pragmatic, public school ideology typically prevailed.

It was therefore the colleges and universities of the western and southern states that most confidently embraced the notion of academic literacy in the vernacular during the first half of the nineteenth century. Meanwhile the eastern schools, and especially the old, privately endowed universities and their preparatory systems, were apt to cling to their classical traditions. This pattern is apparent in Nightingale's 1879 report that 75 percent of all college students in New England were enrolled in a classical course of study, whereas in the Middle Atlantic states of New York, New Jersey, and Pennsylvania, the number declined to 54 percent, and in the sixteen colleges surveyed west and south of Pennsylvania, the number declined even further, to less than 43 percent of the total number of students enrolled.

The same regional pattern with regard to the specification of ancient languages for college admission was still apparent more than thirty-five years later when Kellicott undertook a national survey of college entrance requirements. Noting that the general trend was toward abandoning ancient language study as an admissions requirement, Kellicott reported that the schools west of the Alleghenies were unquestionably the leaders of this movement. While 85.7 percent of the twenty-one New England institutions surveyed specified preparatory work in Latin or Greek, the incidence of the requirement dropped to 79.6 percent among the forty-nine "eastern" institutions to 62.2 percent in thirty-seven southern schools and to 28.9 percent at the ninety-seven western institutions included in the survey (36).

Kellicott's interpretations of the survey findings are interesting for the particular way they foreshadow the debates of the 1920s on the question of whether entrance examinations ought to measure scholastic achievement or aptitude. Kellicott himself perceived the two constructs in terms of *social* versus *educational* standards. The classical language requirement, he explained, derived from the belief that the purpose of higher education was to "conserve certain types of learning and habits of thought regarded as customary and suitable distinctions of an 'upper' leisure class—an intellectual aristocracy." According to his analysis, the requirement that students demonstrate mastery of classical languages for college admission fell into the category of what we would now call an achievement test, for it was designed to ensure that students entering college were already "prepared to receive the stamp of social status which the college proposes to put upon them" (31). Schools that had abandoned the ancient language requirement, on the other hand, embraced what Kellicott referred to as "educational" or "intellectual" as opposed to "social" collegiate standards. Their admissions requirements were aptitude- rather than achievement-oriented, because they looked *forward*—to the students' potential "to undergo and to profit by a more strictly educative process with a view to entering into and sharing in the active life of our democracy" (31).

The inclusive democratic impulses attending both the fall of classical literacy and the rise of English studies in their stead obviously gathered a good deal of their momentum from the western states, where the educational system was dominated by public institutions and where the accreditation system rather than entrance examinations controlled access to higher education. This regional division would continue to characterize the professionalization efforts of English studies departments throughout the nineteenth and much of the twentieth century. By virtue of their greater prestige, the old established eastern schools, though relatively small in number, were able to assume leadership early on in the professionalization process. One of the most influential assertions of the early professional dominance was the New England and Middle Atlantic states' organized drive to articulate nationally standardized college entrance examinations, and inasmuch as they succeeded in the endeavor, the definition of academic literacy that those examinations eventually imposed upon schools across the nation reflects the legacy of the classical heritage of English studies.

In part they achieved this result by drawing upon their tradition of cultural leadership to define western schools and their students as "uncultured" and socially deficient. Davis, for instance, concluded his harsh and lengthy criticism of state universities by conceding that the fault might lie with the "crude" social conditions that made for intellectual deprivation in the western states. "It is possible," he acknowledged, "that some of these difficulties and limitations . . . spring from the crude conditions of the new States, and may be alleviated in a more settled condition of the community and a higher intellectual plane of society" (436). Nearly two decades later, the same vocabulary would prevail in Payne's survey of English studies at American colleges. Noting that the western institutions in the survey were more apt to depart from traditional pedagogies, Payne speculated that the difference might arise from the fact that student populations in the western states presented their English instructors with "cruder material" on which to perform their professional duties.

In the new field of English studies the domination of Ivy League standards was especially pronounced, for the knowledge base of the field was less fixed than that of the other modern subjects. Eventually an established English-language literary canon would supply a considerable degree of field definition that the new discipline needed as the basis for developing a professional identity. And as the entrance examinations featured in chapter 3 demonstrate, that canon formation was primarily the project of the prestigious eastern schools whose reading lists for the college entrance exams in English provided a model soon followed by other schools across the country.

Conscious of the superior social clout of the old established eastern schools and the academic traditions supporting their institutional definitions of literacy, Fred Newton Scott spoke out in 1909 against the strategic advantage the Ivy League colleges enjoyed, even as secondary schools and colleges across the country became increasingly involved in efforts to define the content of English studies by establishing uniform entrance requirements nationwide. Western teachers of English, inclined by the force of their own professional experience to support more pragmatic literacy values, were often silenced by a sense of social inferiority. Thus, as Scott explained, "the attitude of the western teacher has either insensibly conformed to that of the eastern teacher, or has come into more or less embarrassing conflict with it" ("What the West" 11).

Scott was particularly concerned with the Ivy League colleges' insistence upon a pronouncedly literary concept of literacy. Initially this literary emphasis was a manifestation of the achievement-oriented bias of the prestigious private schools that had sought to construct a canon of vernacular texts that could fill the cultural void left by the demise of the classical canon. In constructing such a canon of literary texts to function as the acknowledged receptacles of cultural wisdom, English studies specialists could continue to perform in the role of cultural conservators laid down for them by their predecessors in classical studies.

But this is a subject that receives more detailed attention in chapter 3's study of how entrance examinations have functioned as instruments of canon formation. For now it is sufficient to note that although early attempts to give a literary focus to English studies are typically described as an "impressionistic" movement led by generalists who were out of step with the professionalization process that relied on increasing specialization (see G. Graff), the concept of "literary appreciation" that emerged from this impressionistic approach to English studies strongly influenced formulation of the discipline's notion of professional expertise. Larson describes such an influence as the inevitable effort to define areas of professional knowledge that are not amenable to standardization but are governed by "genius" or "innate talent." The extent to which untutored ability figures in the practices of a profession necessarily changes as the profession becomes a unified community. Inevitably, however, the concept of special talent or charisma is instrumental in the structuring of a hierarchy within the profession as well as in the formulation of criteria for excluding or including potential members (41). As we will see, in the case of English studies, the concept of literary appreciation, signifying an extraordinary sensitivity to the moral and aesthetic virtues of texts, has figured prominently in the definition of a professional knowledge base that is not only highly specialized but that becomes inaccessible to outsiders for other reasons as well.

At the same time that English studies was attempting to build its separate identity upon a foundation of literature- based cultural authority, the more utilitarian working-class demands that fueled the public school ideology needed to be reckoned with, as an industrialized economy began more and more to support the development of vocational studies in the postsecondary curriculum. Liberal studies, because they appeared to have little connection with "real life" fared poorly by comparison with the thriving new vocational courses of study that had been introduced in the colleges and universities. Opportunities for engineers, for example, rose so dramatically by the end of the nineteenth century that the University of Michigan formed a separate school of engineering in 1895 to accommodate a burgeoning student population whose numbers rose from 331 in the first year of the school's existence to 1,165 a mere ten years later. During the same ten years, English studies in Michigan's school of literature increased its enrollment by no more than 300 students (Geiger 14). Roughly the same time period, according to a Harvard presidential report of 1904, saw the liberal arts curriculum making a similarly poor showing against vocational programs at other universities as well. While the number of bachelor's degrees awarded in liberal arts programs at seven colleges surveyed in the Harvard report rose by a full 64 percent between 1890 and 1904, other undergraduate degrees were up 304 percent.

In order to survive such competition for the human and material resources available to higher education, English studies in the American academy needed to define itself not only as a guardian of traditional cultural values but also as a professional discipline with practical virtues, one that could provide an indispensible service to the American people. In part, the early architects of the emerging field of English studies met this requirement by appropriating the values of language study that had held sway in the old classical curriculum. Like the classical languages, it was argued, English could provide the material for rigorous intellectual exercise and discipline. But although the notion that English studies could provide the means of enforcing high intellectual standards held broad appeal to a people indoctrinated with the Protestant work ethic, it was publicity about America's "literacy crisis" near the end of the nineteenth century that established most convincingly the demand for the professional services of English studies specialists.

Harvard's President Eliot was an important force in publicizing the problem and, by way of remedy, instituting the required freshman composition course that for over a century now has been a staple among English department offerings across the country. In his annual report for 1872–73, Eliot paved the way for higher education's entry into the literacy market by publishing examples of student illiteracy gleaned from essays written for the entrance examination, a practice Harvard continued to follow for many years. On the basis of these revelations from the exams, Eliot defined a need for vernacular literacy instruction among college-age students:

> The need for some requisition which should secure on the part of the young men preparing for college proper attention to their own language has long been felt. Bad spelling, incorrectness as well as inelegance of expression in writing, ignorance of the simplest rules of punctuation, and almost entire want of familiarity with English literature, are far from rare among young men of eighteen otherwise well prepared to pursue their college studies. (qtd. in Hays 17–18)

Although Eliot proposed that such fundamental literacy instruction was actually the responsibility of the preparatory schools and fully intended the college freshman composition course he instituted in 1874 to be nothing more than a temporary bridge between the preparatory schools and college, freshman composition soon became ensconsed as a permanent fixture in Harvard's curriculum. As Berlin has observed, by 1894, twenty years after it first appeared in the Harvard catalog, the freshman English course was the single fixed requirement in the college curriculum. By 1897, it was the only two-semester course of study required for graduation (*Rhetoric and Reality* 20).

As the course became more firmly entrenched, and as other colleges and universities began to follow Harvard's example by establishing similar courses in their own curricula, Harvard continued to publish shocking illustrations of student incompetence, and literacy instruction began to be billed across the nation as an indispensable service to the American people. In his introduction to the 1910 book-length survey of English as it was being taught in twenty representative American universities, William Morton Payne, editor for *The Dial,* recorded that the Harvard Report on Composition and Rhetoric was the single most important impetus for bringing the subject of English instruction to the public's attention, making "a burning 'question of the day' out of a matter previously little more than academic in its interest" (12). Payne's account of the wildfire spread of alarm over the nation's literacy crisis as announced by the Harvard report captures the fervor of the times and is worth reproducing at some length:

> The subject was made to reach a larger public than it had ever reached before, and this new and wider public was fairly startled out of its self-complacency by the exhibit made of the sort of English written by young men and women supposed to have enjoyed the best preparatory educational advantages, and to be fitted for entrance into the oldest and most dignified of our colleges. The report was more than a discussion of the evils of bad training; it was an object-lesson of the most effective sort, for it printed many specimen papers *liberatim et verbatim*, and was even cruel enough to facsimile some of them by photographic process.
>
> The seed of discontent having thus been sown broadcast, the field was in a measure prepared for the labors of the English Conference named by the Committee of Ten; and the Report of that Conference, made public early in 1894, has kept the question of English teaching as burning as ever, if, indeed, it has not fanned the flame into greater heat. Not only the educational periodicals, but also many

published in the interests of general culture, and even some of the newspapers—in their blundering way—have kept the subject before the public. Educational gatherings have devoted to it much of their attention, and it has been largely taken up by writers for the magazines. (12–13)

Once word of America's literacy crisis had thus been broadcast beyond the confines of Harvard and like-minded institutions, the possibility was opened for solutions to be offered from sources holding definitions of literacy that differed substantially from those set by Ivy League standards. Within the field of English studies itself, Fred Newton Scott was particularly outspoken against the literacy standards imposed by the eastern schools by means of their examination system. A year before Payne's account of the beneficial effects of Harvard's publicity about a literacy crisis in American education, Scott questioned the formal criteria by which the entrance exams measured literacy, maintaining that a truer measure of literacy was "the crucial test of pragmatism" ("What the West" 18).

Fundamental to Scott's criticism of entrance examinations and formal approaches to literacy instruction was the philosophy of "literacy for life" as opposed to "literacy for school." In an article published in 1901 he had complained of the "feudal" relationship between secondary and college education in the eastern schools where the entrance examination system prevailed. This relationship presupposed that life within the university community had only accidental connection with life in the outside world. Accordingly, preparatory schools were charged with the single task of getting students ready to enter the university, and this meant coaching them to pass the entrance exam. Scott was concerned that the kind of learning that best prepared students for the English exam was memorization of facts and rules—trivia drawn from plots of novels and biographies of famous authors and rules of grammar and punctuation that Scott considered "subsidiary" to the real business of English studies. The true test of students' reading and writing abilities, according to Scott and his fellow "pragmatic philosophers," was their experience in the world outside the academy, and he urged that such a test be applied to the students whose examination papers had been published by the Harvard Committee on English Composition: "Where are they now, the writers of these rejected addresses? Are they in jail? Are they social outcasts? Are they editing yellow journals, or in other ways defiling the well of English? Or are they eloquent preachers, successful lawyers, persuasive insurance agents, leaders of society?" ("What the West" 18–19).

Scott opposed the spectre of standardized entrance examinations fashioned after the Harvard model on the grounds that such exams were hostile to the educational task of promoting the unique development of the student's individual character. The teacher who must always keep one eye upon a set of examination questions while attempting to encourage the growth of students' personalities would eventually cease to educate and begin to "apply the standard of conformity to a more or less conventional requirement" (12).

As future developments in the history of entrance examinations in English studies were to prove, however, the development of individual freedom of expression was by no means the inevitable focus of a pragmatic approach to academic literacy. In actuality, the practical goals of literacy instruction were far more likely to be set by economic constraints and employment opportunities in the outside world than by a humanistic concern for the development and expression of individual character. As the pragmatic concerns of public universities and technical institutes gradually eroded the absolute dominance of the eastern schools, conformity to the requirements of corporate capitalism became, in many ways, as powerful a mandate as the conformity to formal conventions of language use that Scott had opposed at the turn of the century.

This academic responsiveness to the demands of the nation's economic structure is embedded in the curious compromise that emerged from attempts to resolve the east-west conflict over the academic conceptualization of literacy. As chapter 3 will show, the eastern schools' predisposition to invest literacy with the social values attached to high culture led them to champion a belletristic version of literacy that relied heavily upon the ability of candidates to demonstrate mastery of a prescribed body of formal knowledge—the formal characteristics of Standard Written English (particularly in the academic genre of theme writing) and a textual knowledge of the English literary canon. With the examination system of admissions, the eastern schools institutionally enforced the notion that literacy signified academic *achievement*.

For their part, the western schools advanced the public school philosophy of education for life, investing literacy with functional value, as a set of knowledge and skills that equipped individuals to function as informed participants in a democracy. In keeping with their emphasis on developing the potential of students to function productively in the world outside of the academy, their construction of academic literacy was that of *aptitude* rather than achievement, and this they enforced institutionally through the accreditation system. The system presented no specific knowledge requirement as the basis for admission to higher education, but rather asked that students be able to demonstrate through past successes in the academic system that they could profit from further education. Literary studies, an achievement-based branch of English studies, tended to take a backseat to composition, which was valued not as an end in itself but as a means by which both academic and nonacademic ends might be achieved.

During the first two decades of the twentieth century, the rise of pragmatic educational ideals posed a serious threat to the dominance of a literary version of academic literacy, and this pragmatism was increasingly focused upon the goal of successful economic competition. Scott himself, though he wrote glowingly of composition instruction's potential for promoting the healthy development of the student's unique personality, seemed to regard occupational success as the true test of schooling. Indicative of the widespread acceptance of Scott's position on this matter is the following quotation from Robert J. Aley's article on "The College and the Freshman," which appeared in *School and Society* in 1915:

> Higher education is no longer the luxury of a few. Neither is it secured merely as a matter of culture. To the great majority of people higher education is simply more education and is sought because it is believed that its possession will make the individual a more efficient member of the social world and will enable him more readily to meet the fierce competition of modern life. (152)

But although the pragmatic version of literacy advanced here had seriously undermined the literary bias of the private eastern colleges and their followers throughout the country, it was the examination system of the eastern schools that ultimately emerged from the clash between east and west and survived to enjoy national prominence in the regulation of college admissions. In English studies, although their emphasis on literary knowledge was subverted by the triumph of an educational philosophy valuing aptitude over achievement, the examinations, by their very nature, continued to measure formal rather than functional aspects of literacy. And, as the close examination of verbal aptitude portions of the SAT in chapter 5 will demonstrate, the medium of standardized tests such as these itself promotes a formal definition of literacy, objectifying it in such a way that it appears to be a rationally based, socially and politically neutral set of skills. The understanding of academic literacy implicit in such exams is one in close accord with Ohmann's 1976 description of the subject matter of English studies as it emerges from the pages of composition and rhetoric textbooks that "operate without a stated analysis of literacy in technological society and without a politics" (*English* 147). Moreover, as James Berlin has joined Ohmann in arguing, a definition of literacy as an objectifiable set of conventions and rational skills that can be examined and measured in isolation from the social context in which it occurs—a definition implicit in the modern-day descendents of the College Board's first aptitude tests—is in perfect accord with the interests of corporate capitalism. In describing what he terms the "current traditional" rhetoric of the American academy, Berlin could as well be discussing the medium constraints of modern aptitude testing upon the conceptualization of academic literacy:

> Current-traditional rhetoric dictates that certain matters
> cannot be discussed because they are either illusory—not
> empirically verifiable—or they cannot be contained within
> acceptable structures—rational categories, for example.
> This very exclusion, meanwhile, encourages a mode of be-
> havior that helps students in their move up the corporate
> ladder—correctness in usage, grammar, clothing, thought,
> and a certain sterile objectivity and disinterestedness."
> (*Writing Instruction* 75)

In short, even over the relatively brief time span encompassed by the history of efforts to institutionalize national standards of literacy, we see that the identity of the "ruling class" whose values are both reflected and enforced by the practice of literacy testing has changed radically. Those whose interests initially dominated the scene were inheritors of an aristocratic valuation of literacy that had previously found expression in the social exclusivity of the classical curriculum, but they were eventually forced to compromise that definition before the democratic ideals of an expanding public education system. In time, however, the academic authority that representatives of both private and public philosophies struggled to gain came under the control of economic agencies outside the academy itself.

For English studies professionals the progression was marked by drastic revisions in faculty relations with college administration. In the first half of the nineteenth century, the earliest professors of English studies were typically clergymen, and as such they directly participated in carrying out the original mission of higher education in America—the production of cultural leaders. But as Clyde Barrow has pointed out, between 1860 and 1930 the administrative boards of the major private northeastern universities underwent a transformation process. Initially dominated by clergymen, the governing boards by 1930 were controlled by corporate officials from the major financial agencies in America. These corporate board members were inevitably affected by their own occupational outlooks as they steered the course of American higher education, and largely through their agency the corporate model, emphasizing social efficiency and rational decision making, took hold of universities. By 1920, boards of trustees at colleges and universities across the country were dominated by businessmen with "no special competence to pass judgment on matters of educational policy" (Barrow 171). Nevertheless, the boards were accorded the right to guard the financial interests of their institutions even when those interests were affected by educational policies such as admissions standards.

Institutionally, then, the professional identity of English studies specialists, like that of other academicians, was made subservient to corporate interests. Accordingly, the phenomenon of academic standardization initiated by English studies specialists in the late nineteenth century was itself an early manifestation of corporate values, for it facilitated mass production and the introduction of technology into the production process. As we will discover in the chapters that follow, the evolution of standardized literacy testing at the college entry level has proceeded from regionally based internal efforts to establish the canon of English studies' professional knowledge base to external concern for the precise measurement and control of the "essential product" of education. Through the stages of this process, though the nature of the product itself has changed, the market demand for literacy instruction as a professional service has consistently depended upon the time-honored educational practice of "teaching to the test."

CHAPTER THREE

Early Steps Toward Standardizing Literacy as a Professional Product

The task of coordinating a variety of separate educational systems into one was crucial to the professionalization process undertaken by English studies personnel. Not only was the structure of a single, unified educational system essential to the enterprise of standardizing literacy as a professional product, but it provided in addition the necessary institutional means by which the emerging class of academic professionals could control the production of other professionals like themselves as well as the market for their professional services. As I suggested in chapter 2, many of the steps toward establishing the unbroken continuum of a single educational system were directed by the Ivy League schools that, by virtue of their long-established tradition of cultural leadership, were venerated as the arbiters of American educational standards. Since those standards were articulated in the form of college entrance requirements, however, they were increasingly challenged from a variety of perspectives so that the influence of the old established eastern schools was, in the course of time, tempered and redirected by resistance from such entities as public secondary schools, western colleges and universities, and scientifically oriented research institutions. In short, multiple influences and perspectives have contributed to the establishment of educational uniformity and the development of what Cook-Gumperz has termed a "monolithic" definition of academic literacy that has taken shape over the course of the past 100 years.

In this chapter I will trace the development of a standardized definition of academic literacy through the early progress of the movement to establish and enforce standardized college entrance examinations in English. As the movement spread southward and westward from its birthplace in the New England and Middle Atlantic states, the influence of the prestigious Ivy League colleges grew increasingly susceptible to modification by populist demands of a pragmatic nature and a vocational bent. In terms of English studies' professional identity, then, the process of gaining national control over the distribution of academic literacy has entailed considerable redefinition of the cognitive basis of professional knowledge from which derive the criteria for professional inclusion and exclusion.

Successive stages in the early decades of the redefinition process are recorded primarily in English entrance examinations that can be described as "essay tests" or "direct assessment" instruments, the type of exams with which I am chiefly concerned in this chapter. The reign of this type of entrance exam essentially came to an end during the late 1920s, when "objective" or "new type" examinations were introduced as an expedient and scientific means of selecting individuals from applicant pools that were, for the first time in history, too large for colleges to accommodate with their existing facilities. This secondary stage in the history of academic literacy as it has been articulated in college entrance exams provides the subject for chapter 4. For now, however, I turn my attention to an earlier portion of the historical record—that of the late nineteenth century when the traditional examination method of setting entrance standards that originated with the eastern colleges underwent a process of regional standardization and shortly thereafter entered into competition with the new alternative accreditation system gaining prominence in the western states.

The mechanism of entrance examinations was itself a carryover from the classical era when preparatory students were required to demonstrate their mastery of classical texts and languages before they would be granted admission to college. Those examinations essentially controlled the preparatory curriculum, wherein all of a student's courses were directed toward the goal of passing the entrance exam. It should be noted that the early entrance examinations represented a knowledge requirement rather than an educational one. That is, students did not have to complete a specified number of courses or spend a designated number of years in a preparatory school before they could take a college entrance exam; they simply needed to be able to demonstrate their possession of a requisite body of knowledge by performing satisfactorily on the entrance examination. For the most part, "mastery" of this knowledge could be gained through memorization. While the classical curriculum was still in place, this meant the memorization of mathematical tables, vocabulary terms, and the rules governing Greek and Latin grammar, as well as prescribed passages from works of the classical canon.

Because the entrance requirement was knowledge specific and did not assume any particular educational credentials, students who attended the early American colleges typically entered at an age a good two to four years younger than is now the case. In theory, until well into the nineteenth century, individuals who wanted to obtain a college education did not need to have any formal preparatory education at all, though in practice this was rarely the case. Students who received a preparatory education specifically intended to help them pass the entrance exam of a particular college with which the school was closely affiliated held a considerable advantage over those who might prepare for college independently. Increasingly, a costly preparatory education became a virtual prerequisite for admission to the old established colleges in New England and the Middle Atlantic states.

The examination system became the site of serious controversy at about the time when modern subjects entered the colleges toward the end of the nineteenth century, disrupting the uniformity across institutions that had characterized both the college curriculum and entrance requirements for many years. At this juncture, each individual college was free to set its own idiosyncratically revised entrance requirements independently of the rest, resulting in a broad and confusing diversity in entrance examinations among the growing number of colleges then in existence.

Such diversity was a natural consequence of the isolated character of the early colleges. Each college was served by its own small collection of preparatory schools, and a single professor might control all entrance requirements in his department for years. In some cases, because departmental definitions were not firmly established, one professor might even be in charge of designing and administering entrance exams for several subjects (Broome 126–27). As the preparatory schools grew more independent of individual colleges, however, and as the public high schools began to assume an increasing share of the responsibility for college preparatory education, secondary school teachers began to complain that they were unfairly burdened by the diversity of college entrance examinations their students were preparing to take. With students in each graduating class intent upon admission to a wide variety of colleges, each with its own entrance requirements, secondary schools were forced to undertake the expense of holding numerous small classes and were further inconvenienced by having to offer individual tutoring to atone for irregular and superficial work resulting from the fragmentation of classroom instruction.

During the transitional period of curricular change and expansion, English was the subject leading the way in the development of a new set of uniform entrance requirements. The movement began at Harvard, where in 1874 applicants were for the first time required to write a composition in English on a subject taken from a prescribed list of works by standard authors. Almost immediately Harvard's plan to draw English entrance examination questions from a prescribed reading list spread to other colleges in the surrounding area, and in 1879 the Association of Colleges in New England decided to use Harvard's entrance examination in English as the model for English entrance requirements that it hoped would eventually be used uniformly throughout New England.

Until 1884 the movement to promote uniform entrance requirements in English at New England colleges was controlled exclusively by the colleges themselves, though the initial impetus came from students and teachers in the secondary schools. In that year, preparatory school teachers lodged an official protest at the Massachusetts Association of Classical and High School Teachers meeting in Boston, charging that authors and titles on the reading list varied too greatly from year to year and that the reading lists themselves differed considerably from one college to another. The teachers expressed a need for cooperation between secondary school and college teachers in order to ensure common goals and educational continuity between the two academic levels.

Largely through the efforts of that group of teachers, the New England Association of Colleges and Preparatory Schools was formed in 1886. In the same year, thirteen New England colleges formed the Commission of Colleges in New England on Admission Examinations, addressing its attention first of all to the subject of English studies and its problems in developing uniform college entrance requirements. In 1888 a conference of representatives from the two organizations, consisting of both college and high school teachers, made a number of recommendations to the Commission on Admission Examinations, among them the suggestion that there be fewer and less frequent changes in reading lists for the English exams and that there be no substantial increase or decrease in the amount of reading required from year to year. In the same year the majority of New England colleges adopted the commission's reading list, incorporating the conference suggestions into exams for the years 1889 through 1892.

Although the initial steps toward standardization of college entrance requirements in English had been taken, considerable diversity continued to exist among some New England colleges, and even greater lack of uniformity characterized the English requirements of schools outside New England. To address the continuing problem of disparate college entrance requirements and the lack of uniformity in high school English programs, the National Education Association in 1892 appointed a Committee of Ten, which met at Vassar in December of that year. Addressing the question of how the discipline of English studies should define itself, the committee proposed that "the high school course in English should be identical for students who intend to go to college or to a scientific school as for those who do not" and that the English exam "should be made uniform *in kind* throughout the country" but that "uniformity in amount is certainly not practicable and probably not desirable" (NEA, *Report of the Committee of Ten* 93). The committee's specific recommendations include several early points of discussion that were later to become directional markers in the history of relations between literature and composition under the umbrella of English studies. Written expression, the committee maintained, required a knowledge of method that could only be brought into play when the writer was actively demonstrating a knowledge of content. In the English exam, according to the committee's recommendations, that content was properly drawn from topics of literary history or criticism or from passages cited from works on the prescribed reading list.

Because skill in the methodology of writing extended beyond the province of English studies, the Committee of Ten urged that applicants' "ability to write English" be judged on the merits of their performance on the written exams in other subjects as well as English. At the same time, however, the committee accorded legitimacy to

English studies' claims on literacy as the product of specialized instruction by underlining the primacy of the exam in "English language and literature" as an indicator of literacy skills. "The Conference feels strongly," they wrote, "that no student should be admitted to college who shows in his English examination . . . that he is very deficient in ability to write good English" (qtd. in Hays 26).

In 1893, the New England movement to enforce uniformity in college entrance requirements in English was joined by the formation of the Association of College and Preparatory Schools of the Middle States and Maryland. At its first meeting at Columbia the association appointed its own Committee of Ten to study existing entrance requirements in English and to present a recommended plan for bringing uniformity to these requirements. In accomplishing this task, the newly formed Committee of Ten consulted with the Commission of Colleges in New England on Admission Examinations and with the New England Association of Colleges and Preparatory Schools. A joint meeting of committees from all three organizations led to the formation of the first National Conference on Uniform Entrance Requirements in English in 1894. The conference recommended a two-part entrance examination in English, one part featuring composition on topics drawn from a list of ten prescribed books and the other part featuring an essay to be written upon the form, structure, and subject matter of a work or works selected from a second reading list prescribed for study and practice.

Shortly thereafter the movement toward uniform entrance requirements in English began to shed its regionalism and assume a truly national character. Subsequent meetings of the National Conference on Uniform Entrance Requirements in English in 1895 and 1897 drew representatives from the South and from North Central states as well as from New England and the Middle Atlantic region. During the same period Yale, which for years had maintained the anomalous position of requiring no English for admission, joined its neighboring colleges in specifying a requirement in British and American literature (previously classified at Yale as an "aesthetic subject"). In 1894 Yale administered its first entrance examination on an independently compiled list of ten works by British and American authors, but the list met with harsh and immediate criticism from both secondary and college teachers. In response to this censure, Yale in 1895 adopted the New England commission's reading list, and the following year examined its applicants on the works included on the list published by the National Conference on Uniform Entrance Requirements in English.

By the end of the nineteenth century, uniformity had been established more thoroughly on paper than in fact. Hays's study of the period demonstrates the actual lack of uniformity with its report that in 1899 "not more than half of the colleges in the North Atlantic States used the English requirement that they had accepted, and those using it interpreted and applied it, each after his own fashion" (33). To remedy this situation representatives from the colleges and secondary schools of the Middle Atlantic states and Maryland formed the original College Entrance Examination Board (CEEB), whose first examination in June, 1901, was hailed as a means not simply of establishing uniform entrance requirements but of enforcing them as well.

Most of the institutional machinery for standardizing the definition of academic literacy originated with the eastern schools and colleges where the classical tradition of private schooling had long been in place, but the influences of this tradition did not go unchallenged as the standardization movement spread across the nation under the auspices of the CEEB in the twentieth century. Particularly among the public schools west of the Alleghenies there developed a concern that the definition of academic literacy proposed by the entrance requirements of the eastern colleges was too esoteric, too controlled by concern for achievement as opposed to academic aptitude, and too concentrated on formal features rather than functional uses of literacy.

Before we examine the charges and the consequences they had for the formulation of a standard definition of academic literacy, however, it is necessary to have a clear sense of the language studies backgrounds from which both the "eastern" and "western" varieties of literacy developed. The following discussion attempts to facilitate this understanding by presenting some representative examination questions from a variety of colleges not directly involved in the standardization movement during the years surrounding the turn of the century. As the examinations reveal, the field upon which English studies staked its initial academic claims was dominated by the formal concerns of linguistics and philology. As classical language studies yielded their reign to modern language studies during the nineteenth century, linguistic formalism provided an important link between the old academy and the new.

Philological Origins of Vernacular Literacy in the Academy

With the dissolution of the academic community in which classical languages served as the repository of cultural knowledge, the study of Greek and Latin grammar and texts relied more and more heavily on memoriter learning. This trend was accompanied by a growing sense that this kind of memory work, the rote learning of classical texts and of the grammatical paradigms of classical languages, was an end in itself. Gradually the ability to conjugate Latin verbs, for instance, came to be valued more for mental discipline than for the access such knowledge provided into the worlds of Virgil or Cicero. Because this interest in linguistic form was among the last survivors of the deposition of classical language studies, its influence was prominent in the early stages of the rise to power of modern language studies, as was the fact that during the reign of the classical curriculum, English made its primary appearances only as a language into which Greek and Latin could be translated. The persistent presence of linguistic formalism through the academy's transfer of attention from classical to modern language studies is witnessed by the single focus of the very first entrance examinations in English (Princeton, 1819; Yale, 1822) on matters of spelling, punctuation, capitalization, grammar, prosody, sentence and paragraph construction, and other formal or mechanical features of written language.

At first, such examinations were oral, not written. Eventually, however, written form gained prominence as students were more and more required to produce short answers in writing to questions such as the following, which comprised the entire 1870 entrance examination in English grammar at Illinois Industrial University (now the University of Illinois at Urbana-Champaign). Although as an "industrial" university Illinois subscribed to a strong vocational sense of its educational mission, it is interesting to note that English in this examination betrays its academic heritage as a translation language and is approached almost as a foreign language might be.

The exam does not require students to read or compose in English, but simply to describe its rules and its irregularities:

1. Name the vowells; the labials; the dentals; the palatals.
2. Define Etymology; the name and different classes of words.
3. Give the different modes of expressing gender in English—illustrate each.
4. Give four rules for the formation of the plural of nouns, and an example under each.
5. Give the rules for the formation of the possessive case of names; and write the possessive plural of *lady, man, wife.*
6. Give the distinction between personal and relative pronouns.
7. What are auxiliary verbs? Name them.
8. Give the third-person singular of the verb *sit* in all the tenses of the indicative mood.
9. He said that that that that that pupil parsed was not that that he should have parsed. Parse the *that's* in this sentence.
10. He that cometh unto me I will in no wise cast out. Between you and I there is much mischief in that plan. I intended last year to have visited you.

   Correct these sentences, and give four reasons for your corrections.

(Illinois Industrial University, "Examination Questions for Honorary and Prize Scholarships for 1870")

Throughout the remainder of the nineteenth century, academic emphasis on prescriptive rules and formal correctness of English language usage is recorded in entrance examinations that continued to require the nearly exclusive attention of students to these and similar linguistic features and systems. As Gerald Graff has pointed out, the same period saw the steady growth of literary studies within the field of English, but well into the twentieth century, English and American literature served as little more than source material for the essays students wrote to gain admission to college. In 1874, when Harvard initiated the practice of publishing a reading list of literary works from which the following year's English entrance exam questions would be drawn, the applicant's demonstrated understanding or appreciation of literature did not appear among the published criteria that would be used in evaluating the essay responses. The description of that exam published in the 1874 Harvard *Catalog* clearly indicates the extent to which the literacy values of the English department continued at that time to be influenced by the philological origins of English studies. Under the heading "English Composition," the *Catalog* description explains, "Each candidate will be required to write a short *English Composition*, correct in spelling, punctuation, grammar, and expression, the subject to be taken from such works of standard authors as shall be announced from time to time" (qtd. in Hays 18).

These and similar criteria continued to be the dominant concerns of English examinations at Harvard and at the many colleges and universities throughout the country where the Harvard model was used during the last quarter of the nineteenth century. The typical college entrance examination in English at major American colleges during the late 1800s required students to read a number of works appearing on a prescribed reading list. The literary works would then furnish the subject matter for essays, but although examinees were occupied with composing texts, the texts would be evaluated almost exclusively by their adherence to the same sorts of formal rules of mechanics and usage that the Illinois exam called upon students to describe.

The Harvard influence was widespread, extending well beyond the New England and Middle Atlantic states that initiated its transformation into public policy. In a very short time, entrance examinations in English patterned after the 1874 Harvard model were used in many of the important colleges across the United States. Certainly the published descriptions of entrance examinations in English provided by such colleges throughout the country during this era indicate that a candidate's successful performance depended less on mastery of the literary subject matter than on mastery of the conventions of standard written English.

Typical of a great many entrance examinations in English during this time were those administered at the University of Texas at Austin. Like Harvard, the University of Texas required its students to write an essay in response to a question drawn from a literary work on a prescribed reading list. From its opening in 1883 until 1891, the university's published descriptions of the criteria by which these examination essays would be evaluated listed only "neatness, spelling, capitalization, punctuation, paragraphing, and grammatical correctness" (see the 1885–86 *Catalogue* 86–87). No mention of subject matter is made until 1914, with the exception of the 1891–92 and 1896–97 examination instructions that add the explanatory note, "The entire paper will be graded on neatness, capitalization, punctuation, paragraphing, grammar, and subject matter" (1891–92 *Catalogue* 60). "Subject matter" reappeared as an evaluation criterion in the University of Texas examination instructions in 1914 and remained there until 1920, when the university began to subscribe to the College Board exams. Before 1914, however, evaluation of the entrance exam in English at Texas continued, with only occasional and slight modifications, to be based on the set of formal criteria described in the 1892–93 *Catalogue*:

> The main test will consist in writing upon a given subject, a composition, correct in spelling, punctuation, capitalization, grammar, sentence construction, and paragraphing. The written examination may be supplemented by oral questions upon particular points such as peculiarities in the forms of plurals and in various kinds of syntactical agreement. (15)

At the University of Texas, as at many other colleges across the country, questions similar to those described here as likely to appear on the oral part of the exam soon became a written portion of the test, intended to supplement the essay. At Harvard, in fact, such questions, hearkening back to the pre-1874 entrance exams, were reinstated in 1882 as a half-hour written supplement to the major essay portion of the exam. For the next twenty years, these supplemental questions in the Harvard entrance exam, and likewise in the exams at most of the important New England colleges and universities, required students to correct specimens of "bad English" (Hays 19–20).

While the writing of an essay provided evidence of the examinee's ability to put a perhaps unconscious knowledge of formal linguistic rules into practice, short-answer questions such as those that might have appeared on Harvard's supplemental section or on the oral portion of the 1893–94 University of Texas exam, on the other hand, required a meta-linguistic awareness—an ability not only to use but to describe the linguistic rules that govern the writing of standard, academic English. Plainly the emphasis of such questions was not on the purposeful use of grammatical or mechanical rules—to reduce ambiguity for the reader, for instance—but rather on the rules as ends in and of themselves. Accordingly, such supplemental questions typically required students to demonstrate their knowledge of language structures and conventions in isolation from actual written discourse.

The effect of such emphasis on the formal construction of English is to complicate and "exoticize" the familiar and thus to present the knowledge of the vernacular as a suitably specialized professional skill. The subject matter of English studies is further elevated from the lowly position it held as the vernacular during the classical era, when mastery of English was not considered to require formal study, by the arcane vocabulary employed in its description; it becomes a specialized academic subject when it can be talked about in specialized academic terms. The requirement that prospective college students be able to converse about English according to these academic specifications is apparent on the short-answer supplement to the essay examination published in the "Specimen Paper" section of the *University of Texas Catalogue*, 1894–95 (by which time, the short-answer questions had become part of the written entrance examination in English):

1. Decline: *she, boy, ally, mouse, princess, Frenchman.*

2. Synopsize the verb *seek* in the Indicative Mood.

3. Name and illustrate the various uses in English of (1) the Participle and (2) the Gerund.

4. Briefly parse the italicized words: (1) Seek *to do well.* (2) James, the *postman, having brought me a letter,* I am happy. (3) I hear *that* you come *to study philosophy.* (4) *Reaching Austin Thursday,* we registered at the Driskill. (5) *To sing* this *song* is delightful. (6) I am six *feet* tall, but not a *Kentuckian.*

5. Write correctly: (1) Can I go to town. Or will I stay at home. (2) He begs to draw their attention to the fact that owing to having almost the exclusive sale of books used in the College enables him to buy largely, and thereby to give the best discount. (3) We the undersigned electors of austin knowing that you have been prominently connected with the interests of the city for many years, and also a large tax-payer, we deem you admirably fitted to represent us at the council board. (4) I came last week. Reaching here Thursday.

6. What is a paragraph? How is it indicated in writing and in printing?

The practice of dividing examination questions into those that tested applicants' abilities to identify and describe the conventions of academic English and those that tested their abilities to apply the conventions in their own writing soon became standard at most colleges and universities throughout the country. On the West Coast, the University of California at Berkeley, for example, also included such a section of short-answer questions about formal rules and the terms used to describe them, but while Texas drew the subjects for its examples from contemporary life in the university community, thus making an apparent distinction between that part of the exam and the literary essay portion, which drew its subject matter from the works on the prescribed reading list, Berkeley often used literary material in both types of question. In June of 1891, for instance, the entrance exam in English at Berkeley presented examinees with a twenty-five-line passage of poetry and posed the following questions:

(a) Give a full grammatical account of the words italicized.

(b) Analyze the second sentence.

(c) Point out and explain the rhetorical figures found in the passage.

(d) Assign the passage to its poem and place.

A final question, unrelated to the poetry passage, asks students to "discuss, as fully as you can, the principles of sentence structure, illustrating by correct and faulty sentences" (*University of California Admission Circular,* 1891, 42).

Berkeley's nearly exclusive focus on literary material as the basis of its exam questions—both short-answer and essay—seems at first glance to indicate a firm commitment to the notion that English studies is essentially literary studies. In fact, however, Berkeley, like Texas and the majority of leading colleges and universities of the period, placed minimal emphasis on its applicants' demonstrated understanding or appreciation of literary texts. Although the essay portion of the exam invariably drew its questions from prescribed works of literature, instructions to students about that part of the exam typically make no specifications of content. Points of style, arrangement, and formal correctness, on the other hand, receive considerable attention.

From 1881 through 1890, for example, the instructions accompanying Berkeley's entrance exam in English stipulate that the essay must be written "in as finished and perfect a literary form as you can command," and on the June 1891 exam are added to this stipulation the instructions "observe due proportion in the parts of your composition" (*University of California Admission Circular,* 1893, 41). A more precise indication of what constitutes "perfect literary form" and "due proportion" appears in the 1905 exam instructions, which explain that candidates are to choose essay subjects from lists of literary topics and "write thereon a paper neat, legible, and correct in grammar and spelling." The instructions go on to say that "the paper will not be rated so much on accuracy of knowledge involved as upon organization of thought and effectiveness of expression" (*University of California Bulletin,* "Entrance Exam in Subject A (English)," 1905, n. pag.).

The universities of Texas and California were certainly not unique in emphasizing form and correctness in their English entrance examinations at the turn of the century. They were instead representative of the large state universities founded in the midnineteenth century whose policies and standards were at first loosely fashioned after those of the Ivy League colleges. Nor was it only the state universities where this prescriptive emphasis on the formal properties of written language prevailed. Private religious colleges such as St. Ignatius College (founded in Chicago in 1880 and later to become Loyola University), even though they did not directly adopt the Harvard plan of drawing essay questions from literary texts, shared the same emphasis on formal conventions of written English. In 1905, the *Catalogue* description of entrance exams at St. Ignatius lists only four subjects in which students were required to submit to examination for admission. Derived from the core curriculum of the classical academy, these four subjects, with the exception of arithmetic, were all language based: English grammar, original composition, reading, and arithmetic. Topics to be covered in the English grammar examination included etymology, rules of syntax, corrections of false syntax with reasons, parsing, and analysis of sentences. The original composition exam was concerned with "punctuation, spelling, and use of capital letters" (*St. Ignatius College Catalogue,* 1905, 26). Literature entered into entrance requirements only as oral performance; for their examination in reading, applicants were asked to read "at sight" from works that more often than not were literary classics (26).

Finally, the prescriptive formalist conception of literacy at the college entrance level during that time is apparent also in the entrance examinations of some nonstate public schools, such as the Free Academy (later City College) of New York. Founded in 1847 to provide citizens of New York City with access to free public higher education, the Free Academy, like St. Ignatius, rejected the Harvard model of the English entrance exam, and in so doing, almost entirely excluded literature from the notion of English studies that emerges from the exam.

In 1883, for example, the examination in English for admission to the Free Academy consisted of six parts, only one of which entailed the writing of an essay. The first of those parts was a sentence-combining exercise, apparently designed to test mastery of such grammatical principles as subordination and parallelism. The second section required examinees to correct errors of agreement, word order, and inflection in given sentences and to provide a reason for each correction. The third part of the exam asked students to "name but not analyze" examples of sentences (periodic, suspended, etc.), while the fourth section required them to name a lengthy complex sentence and analyze it in terms of "chief parts with their relation or dependence." The fifth section required students to parse words in a sentence consisting of six lines of poetry, explaining the relation and dependence of these words. And the sixth and final section asked examinees to compose a description, no less than fifteen lines long, of the Brooklyn Bridge, being careful to mention six points that were specified on the exam. Instructions to students regarding this final section caution them that "penmanship, punctuation, the use of capitals, and neatness of arrangement" rather than factual knowledge are to be tested in the final exercise (College of the City of New York [1883], *Examinations for Admission, English,* n. pag.).

East Versus West: Regional Biases in the Form Versus Function Conflict

Although philological and mechanical concerns dominated the early years of English studies in America, the field gradually annexed to its holdings the terrain of literary studies, a development that effectively completed the replacement of classical literacy with a distinctly academic variety of the vernacular. As Graff's institutional history of literary studies points out, as long as Greek and Latin texts constituted the accepted body of academic knowledge, English literature found its place in nonacademic settings. Unlike the classical texts, English literature could be read and enjoyed without requiring particular intellectual exertion; it was a source of diversion rather than study—a "feminine" analogue to the "masculine" rigors of classical studies. In addition, throughout much of the nineteenth century, English literature retained a pronouncedly oral character that contributed to its social as opposed to its academic valuation. Providing the texts for oral readings in social gatherings, English literature was for a long time more closely associated with the primarily extracurricular elocutionary culture on campuses than with the academic curriculum.

The earliest efforts on the part of the emerging departments of English to appropriate literature for the task of building a separate, professional knowledge base are recorded in entrance examinations that use literary works as source material for applicants' demonstration of their philological understanding. In 1866, Harvard introduced literary texts into the examination process by requiring prospective students to read aloud from selected works of Shakespeare and Milton. By 1874, however, the oral requirement had assumed written form in an entrance examination that prescribed a canon of literary texts for students to master—largely through memorization and recitation—in order to prepare themselves for college admission. The first prescribed list was short, containing only five works by three English authors: Shakespeare's *The Tempest, Julius Caesar*, and *The Merchant of Venice*; Goldsmith's *The Vicar of Wakefield*; and Scott's *Lay of the Last Minstrel*. During the next five years Harvard's reading list grew steadily, and by 1879 it contained a total of nine works, representing six English authors.

At first, however, the developing literary nature of English studies was probably more apparent on paper than in practice. Despite the fact that literary texts alone provided the source material for examination questions, the catalog description of Harvard's entrance exam in English appeared under the heading "English Composition." The distinction, which the discipline currently insists upon, between composition and literature was not clearly delineated at the time of the early exams, as is evidenced by Eliot's description of "systematic study of the English language" in the 1872–73 report, where "familiarity with English literature" is classified together with spelling, punctuation, and correct and elegant expression as an indicator of students' "proper attention to their own language."

Eliot's decision to include literature on that list, however, lay the groundwork for the development of literary studies as an independent branch of professional knowledge. The 1872–73 report resulted in Harvard's decision to revise the traditional examination form in 1874, replacing short-answer questions about grammar and usage with an essay question on a literary topic. But even though the revised form of the exam purportedly united literature and language study in the medium of written composition, the union was not solid enough to prevent a division of the test into separate sections on literature and language (i.e., grammar, usage, penmanship, mechanics) a mere eight years later.

For more than a decade following Harvard's separation of composition from literature in the form of a sentence-correction supplement to the essay exam, college and high school associations on the East Coast debated the value of the supplemental section. Finally, in 1894 the National Conference on Uniform Entrance Requirements in English resolved the controversy by voting against the inclusion of such an exercise among uniformly sanctioned admissions requirements. With its decision the National Conference took an important step toward endorsing literature as the primary focus of English studies at the college entry level. Its conception of English studies was eagerly embraced by a majority of college and secondary teachers in the East. At that time the National Conference, in actuality a regional organization whose members came exclusively from New England and the Middle Atlantic states, gave official voice to the popular concensus among English teachers of the region that their professional duties transcended the mere teaching of clear and correct written expression. In effect, their position advocated the overthrow of a potentially pragmatic, or functionally based, rhetorical course of professional development in favor of one governed by an aesthetic, or formally based, poetic (see Berlin, *Rhetoric and Reality* 1).

As literary studies began to establish a place for itself in the curriculum, the schools subscribing to the notion that literacy for college-bound students necessarily entailed knowledge and appreciation of an emerging literary canon typically advanced their support of a belletristic version of literacy on moral as well as intellectual grounds. At the second annual meeting of the Modern Language Association in 1886, Franklin Carter's defense of "Modern Languages in Our Higher Institutions" was representative of the growing sense that modern literature was better suited than classical literature to elevate an individual above the concerns of the masses. The function of modern language study, he testified, was to take over the classical languages' task of promoting high culture, and in accordance with the value of his subject matter, the modern language instructor was engaged in a noble calling. "To lift [students] into the spontaneous consideration of the true, the beautiful in thought, and the study of the development of character as related to these other elements is a noble service," Carter insisted, and the conscientious performance of that service could "fit a young man, make him able and intellectually worthy to hold converse with the great" (19).

The belief that literary study was morally elevating and essential to the development of finely tuned sensitivity was not confined exclusively to the eastern seaboard, but in fact was subscribed to by aspiring English studies professionals across the country as a way of justifying their subject matter. That argument became less effective in the western states, however, as industrialization advanced and higher education in the state universities grew increasingly vocational. The tension that developed at many of the western institutions between pragmatic values and the literary conceptualization of English studies they inherited from the older eastern schools is illustrated with particular clarity in the case of Stanford University, where English studies was initially structured after the Harvard model but later revised to more closely accord with the more utilitarian mission of a research university.

Founded in 1891, Stanford based its original admissions policies on the precedent established by its older, neighboring institution, the University of California at Berkeley. In the years immediately preceding the opening of Stanford, Berkeley had employed an entrance examination in English that adopted the Harvard approach by requiring students to write essays on subjects drawn from a reading list of literary works. Following this example, Stanford, during its first year, likewise required a literary essay from its applicants and allowed them to substitute either the Berkeley or Harvard reading list for the one compiled by English department personnel at Stanford.

A subsequently published review of the first entrance exam in English at Stanford, however, announced the failure of the Harvard type of examination to meet the needs of Stanford and its students. "In theory," wrote H. B. Lathrop, who had conducted the review, the type of examination developed by the New England Association of Colleges and Preparatory Schools was intended to "test the students' command of the English language, and to enforce upon schools the importance of proper instruction in English composition," while its encouragement of literary study was only incidental (290). In practice, however, Lathrop went on to say, the exam encouraged students to concentrate on the study of literature at the expense of practice in composition. Consequently, examiners at Stanford found that students taking the first English entrance exam at their university "were almost invariably unable to write clearly and grammatically, though they knew their books tolerably well" (290).

Further study of secondary school preparation under the New England Association's exam system revealed to the Stanford English faculty the extent to which instruction in composition suffered from the alleged union of composition and literature under the umbrella term of *English studies:*

> Investigation seemed to show that to the minds of teachers
> and pupils alike, acquaintance with the prescribed books

was the main purpose of preparation in English. Practice in writing was casual, hurried, perfunctory. Further, the plan of setting subjects out of books seemed to have the injurious effect of causing teachers to set no subjects in class except out of books. (290)

To correct the perceived shortcomings in secondary English instruction, Stanford radically revised its entrance examination in English, designating literature and composition as separate preparatory studies, subject to separate examinations. Of the two, Stanford chose to emphasize composition as the more essential for college preparation. All applicants to Stanford could satisfy the admissions requirement in literature by presenting certificates from their high schools, but all candidates were required to take an examination to prove proficiency in composition. Under the revised plan, the composition exam itself was dissociated completely from literary form and content. Instead of writing formal essays or themes on subjects drawn from books on a prescribed reading list, students could expect to be asked for compositions in such nonliterary forms as business letters or narratives of personal experience.

It would be inaccurate, of course, to claim that at the turn of the century higher education in the East uniformly and without reservation embraced the literary definition of literacy advanced by the Harvard exam, while all western schools espoused with equal enthusiasm the more pragmatic definition championed by Stanford. The case of the Free Academy of New York City, which scarcely acknowledged literature at all in its entrance exams, indicates that "working class" colleges in the East could be every bit as pragmatic as western schools. Nevertheless, the evidence of college entrance examinations in English supports the general claim of Michigan's Fred Newton Scott (1909) that the schools in the eastern and western United States had come to hold very different ideas about the goals of English studies in high school and college.

In large part, their differences can be explained by the very different student populations being served by schools in the two regions and by the newly established western schools' freedom from the biases of a classical heritage that connected higher education with leisure and social prestige. As Payne observed in 1910, the western schools were virtually compelled to be innovative in their methods of English instruction because the students in attendance were much "cruder" material than those in New England. As a spokesman for Stanford, Lathrop is careful to point out that "American universities do not exist for the sons of gentlemen only" (295) and that very few gentlemen's sons could be found among the students at Stanford. "The students at Palo Alto are poor," he wrote. "They sweep, they cook their own food, they dig and write, some of them laboring five hours a day" (293).

Such students required academic literacy to be something other than a badge of social distinction. What good was a cultured sensitivity to literary effects and an easy familiarity with the masterpieces of English literature to someone who had not the leisure to appreciate and enjoy literature for its own sake? In keeping with the needs and demands of its own student body, then, Stanford, like many of the public colleges and universities west of the Alleghenies, endorsed the pragmatic notion of literacy as a tool for increasing the individual's potential for productive participation in society. In accordance with this belief, Lathrop responded to Eliot's alarm about the American literacy crisis by emphasizing the responsibility of universities to model the philosophy of education for life rather than education for the sake of more education. Lathrop wrote that Stanford shared Harvard's concern for "the shocking illiteracy of American youth" (293), maintaining that by revising its entrance exam Stanford hoped to reform the English studies profession by forcing the public high schools of California to provide more "efficient" instruction in English:

> If many undergraduates at Harvard are sitting in Egyptian darkness, what words can be found to express the depth of benightedness in which the high-school pupils who do not go to any college are plunged? To such pupils the elevation of the standard of entrance to college is a direct and precious gift, and through them to the commuity; for what greater gift can a State receive than an increase in the power and usefulness of its citizens? (295)

The Belletristic Bias in Early Efforts to Standardize College Entrance Examinations in English

Stanford's difficulty with the Harvard model of entrance examination was one many western institutions were simply able to circumvent. Until the early years of the twentieth century, admission to western colleges was regulated almost exclusively by the system of high school certification, leaving many western schools free to promote their own educational ideals and their own standards of literacy with little or no regard for the professional course being steered by the eastern schools. In effect, the western certification system meant substituting an educational requirement for the knowledge requirement of the eastern schools. Any student who had successfully completed the secondary course of study in an accredited high school— one whose curriculum and instruction had been approved by overseers from the state university—was automatically granted admission to the university. Entrance examinations were used only rarely, in the case of out-of-state applicants or individuals whose secondary education had taken place in an unaccredited school.

By the turn of the century, however, the separation of private and public, eastern and western school systems was being increasingly challenged by students who had received their secondary education in the public schools and were seeking admission to the private eastern colleges. Making the transition was often difficult if not impossible, since entrance examinations of the private eastern schools tended to enforce certain fixed requirements—primarily ancient language requirements and the reading of a narrowly prescribed list of literary works—that a public school education had not prepared the student to meet.

Circumstances such as these created a demand for the leveling of regional differences. Toward that end the entrance examination system, already responsible for considerable standardization in the East, found an opportunity for national extension. As we have seen, in the movement toward nationally uniform entrance requirements, the prestige of the Ivy League colleges gave eastern educators a psychological advantage, and western teachers were inclined to defer to their authority. As a result, by 1915, six years after Scott published his complaint that "the attitude of the western teacher has either insensibly conformed to that of the eastern teacher, or has come into more or less embarrassing conflict with it" ("What the West" 11), only one institution east of the Alleghenies, apart from the women's colleges, had adopted the certification approach to college admissions that had originated in the West. Meanwhile, the CEEB, founded as an agency for institutionalizing the eastern system of entrance examinations, was finding a home in many western outposts.

According to Scott, the domination of eastern standards perpetrated the "preparatory fallacy" upon secondary English education by institutionalizing the premise that "the chief purpose of secondary English is to prepare the student to enter the university" (10). Such preparation entailed teaching to the test—coaching students to memorize stock questions and answers and to be able to produce a specific collection of responses as proof of fitness for higher education. Scott described the literacy underlying such requirements as artificial, highly conventionalized, and devoid of emotional vitality and communicative function:

> Books which were read and, we may hope, enjoyed in the Freshman and Sophomore years, and which have now been properly forgotten, must be brought out and laboriously re-read. The answers to the old questions must be committed to memory: Whether the Vicar preferred the blue bed to the brown, and why; the numbers of the *Spectator* in which the Sir Roger de Coverly papers appeared; the color of the gown worn by the cardinal in *Quentin Durwood;* Is a barbarous age more favorable to the production of great poetry than an age of refinement?
>
> It is a dreary process, but what else can be done? To attempt to bring back the first fine careless rapture, if happily there was one, would be absurd. Besides, the entrance requirements do not call for it. They call for facts, or else for delicate critical discriminations, outlines of plots, and pallid little essays on the character of Dunston Cass. ("What the West" 13)

Scott contrasted this version of academic literacy with the pragmatic, functionally oriented one advanced by the western schools where, in composition, communication was emphasized over convention, and in reading, appreciation and response were favored over memorization. Urging educators to "do away with all pretence, affectation, and artificiality" (18), he called for entrance requirements that reinforced the rhetorical value of literacy, in accordance with its function as "the working instrument of the social instinct" (19). In his desire to keep the rhetorical conceptualization of literacy from being subsumed by the profession's growing regard for English as a medium of the poetic impulse, Scott finally advocated the separation of literature and composition into distinct courses of study, claiming that the "artificial alliance" of the two originally came into being simply for the convenience of the examiner and not because of any natural connections between the two studies themselves (14). (Scott's comments in this regard are echoed in Gerald Graff's observation that the use of English literary texts as source material for philological examination questions was a crucial step toward institutionalizing literary study as the cognitive basis of English studies: "The philologists had solved the problem that had perennially thwarted the claim of English literature to be a classroom subject: that you could not examine in it" [73].)

By seeking to liberate composition from the domination of literary studies, Scott and other educators of his kind advanced an understanding of literacy that eventually came to be labeled "scholastic aptitude" as distinct from "achievement" in literary studies. In recent years, of course, scholastic aptitude has gained currency as a label for the "essential product" of formal education in this country. As Richard Snow has explained, to the modern educator, "scholastic aptitude represents skill in the *medium* of formal education" (43), and it is just such a skill that western colleges purported to assess with the accreditation system. In the field of English studies, the developing distinction between aptitude and achievement corresponded to a sharpening delineation between composition and literature and between eastern and western constructions of academic literacy. At the time that Scott was refuting the "preparatory fallacy" and the resulting perception of English studies as a finite body of knowledge that could be "mastered" or "possessed," the essentially epistemic understanding of literacy he himself advocated found little favor among those who were most directly responsible for formulating public policy statements about the nature of professional expertise in the field. Verbal aptitude, unless it could be defined according to rules of correctness, seemed impossible to measure or assess by the examination system that was so firmly entrenched in the East. To a considerable extent the dominance of eastern schools in advancing their own version of academic literacy through the medium of formal examinations can be explained by the long and highly revered educational traditions behind such a system. But additionally, the success of the eastern schools in promoting entrance examinations can be attributed to the fact that the eastern schools were the first to band together to form a centralized authority, the CEEB, which eventually grew capable of regulating the profession's national identity. As subsequent chapters will argue, the CEEB succeeded largely because it was compatible with the organizational structure and the productivity standards upon which the survival of the academic professions had come to depend. By the midtwentieth century, the CEEB had begun to delegate much of the responsibility for designing and administering entrance exams to a separate corporate entity, namely the Educational Testing Service (ETS). In its hands, aptitude testing was perfected according to the corporate ideal of time efficiency and cost-effectiveness. By the time the concept of scholastic aptitude finally came into its own, then, it was far removed from the notion of literacy that Fred Newton Scott had struggled, for the most part unsuccessfully, to promote. Throughout much of the early decades of the twentieth century, the eastern tendency to favor achievement in literary studies directed the development of English entrance examinations. As the College Board's influence spread from its eastern point of origin and the standardization movement gained momentum throughout the country, even independent-minded schools such as Stanford found themselves deferring to the "eastern" biases of a centralized authority. Eventually, subscribing to the College Board's entrance examinations became a virtual requirement for schools that were serious about promoting academic professionalism. And for English studies during the early decades of the century, such a move signified the construction of English studies professional knowledge as literary achievement.

CHAPTER FOUR

Conflicts Between Literature and Composition on the Road from Achievement to Aptitude

The first CEEB English examination, administered in 1901, was essentially designed to measure achievement in the subject of English literature, and its concern for formal English grammar was little more than incidental. The exam established the long-standing pattern of dividing the test into two sections: English A—questions drawn from a list of books specified for *Reading*—and English B—questions drawn from books designated for *Study and Practice*. As the Commission on English's report to the College Board explained in 1931, achievement in English literature as measured by the early two-part CEEB exams was heavily dependent upon the candidate's ability to reproduce factual information and passages of text from memory:

> The examiners apparently at first had no desire to test any specific kind of knowledge or power. In English A in 1901 the candidate was required to write three compositions each covering two pages of the examination book, the three topics to be chosen from a list of twelve. These topics included reproduction, biography, free literary discussion, analysis of character, literary technique, the historical background of a novel or a group of essays, and the history of literature. At least four could have been answered by memoriter reproduction without any further reflection than is required in the condensation and arrangement of material. There was no indication that answers revealing wider knowledge and power would be considered of greater value. In English B the question on grammar was very elementary. The two other questions in English B required only simple reproduction of material in Macaulay's *Essay on Milton* and in Shakespeare's *MacBeth*. (2–3)

In the 1901 exam under discussion here, the English A (Reading) section featured twelve questions about literary texts and their authors. As the commission noted in 1931, satisfactory essay responses to those questions apparently required a good memory for textual features such as plot construction and descriptive details. The first question, for example, asks examinees to recount the action in the fifth act of *The Merchant of Venice;* another question calls for reconstruction of the different stories that are worked together in *Silas Marner;* and another asks examinees to identify two events that changed the course of Silas Marner's life and to explain the direct effect of each. Question 2 in the exam calls for reproduction of character descriptions by asking students to describe the two sides of Achilles as revealed by the *Iliad,* illustrating each and finally telling whether a similar contrast can be found in the character of Hector; question 5 asks for a description of how Hawkeye followed a trail; and question 10 calls for some description of Uncas and Magua, with some accompanying discussion of the degree to which Cooper intends either to be a representative of the typical Indian character.

The dominant rhetorical modes examinees were required to produce in such essays are description and narration, and that is true not only in questions about the literary texts themselves but also in questions that demand some recollected knowledge of the historical background of the texts or biographical information about their authors. Consider, for example, question 4, which asks what picture of eighteenth-century life can be drawn from Addison's Sir Roger de Coverly papers, or question 7, which calls for a composition on "that part of Scott's life in which he wrote the Waverly novels."

Although most of the questions, like those noted above, call for the written reproduction of recollected knowledge, at least one question on the 1901 exam calls for some imaginative speculation. In responding to question 9, asking students to imagine the Princess Ida's possible comment on a speech by Portia to Bassanio, the student must imaginatively enter into the character of Scott's Ida in order to respond to Portia's words. The presence of that particular question in the 1901 exam testifies that the College Board's concern with factual recall was not as exclusive as the commission's report seems to imply. Indeed, the question requires students to adopt a reader's stance that in western academic tradition is fundamental to the appreciation of distinctly literary texts—the willing suspension of disbelief. In order to respond as the character of Ida, the reader must accept that such a character actually exists, not merely as a construction of words on a page but as an actual living human being capable of emotional and intellectual responses to new situations. Moreover, the reader must be able to empathize with such a character in order to predict what her responses might be to these new circumstances. In essence, then, the question blurs distinctions between literature and life and assumes that examinees are able to "fictionalize" themselves as "literary" readers (see Ong, *Interfaces*).

While questions of this sort were admittedly rare in the early years of the College Board's English examinations, they became more common and less constrained by specific texts as time passed. By 1915, the College Board made a significant move toward testing for aptitude rather than literary achievement by publicizing its intention to test "power" as well as students' abilities to recall specific information contained in the prescribed texts. The term *power* as it was defined by the National Conference on Uniform Entrance Requirements in English signified "thinking" and "appreciation" as opposed to "mere memorizing" (Leonard 298). As the conference proceedings for 1915 indicated, educators had come to believe that the early emphasis on memorization imposed an "unnatural and deadening drill" upon classroom procedures and was so time-consuming that "other more vital English studies are crowded out of the school course" (298).

In an effort to shift emphasis from memory to power, the board devised a new examination option, the Comprehensive Examination in English, which was first administered in 1916. Once again the inspiration for the board's innovation came from Harvard, which at the time was still independently administering its own entrance exams. In 1911 Harvard had introduced its "new plan" of admission— a plan featuring a revised English examination that, instead of testing an applicant's mastery of certain books, was designed to measure "kinds and degrees of attainment" (Greenough 374) and to examine the student's "power to write, power to think, and power to read and appreciate" (Leonard 298). Unlike earlier exams, the 1911 Harvard exam was not tied to a specific, prescribed reading list, but rather it gave students and secondary teachers considerable freedom to determine the reading background that would best prepare students to demonstrate their powers of writing, thinking, reading, and appreciation of literature. The 1911 exam at Harvard therefore contained a number of questions that, although they required very specific responses, could be answered "from almost any possible list of reading" (Greenough 373). Examples of such questions are included in the following, drawn from the June 1911 exam at Harvard:

1. Select from any play which you have read an important character who has one marked weakness and show into what difficulties this weakness leads him.

2. Quote twenty consecutive lines of poetry and then tell very briefly why you think them good poetry.

3. Suppose a public library, wishing to interest people in good reading, to be composing brief descriptive lists of novels and essays. Suppose the first note to have run thus: "*Treasure Island*, by Robert Louis Stevenson: An exciting romance of the sea, pirates, buried treasure, and other adventures. Vivid descriptions of both scenes and persons. John Silver, the cook, is one of the great characters in English prose fiction." Write similar brief descriptive notes for any three novels or books of essays that you have read, whether on the prescribed list or not.

8. Have you ever read a book which you enjoyed more than any of the books on the prescribed list? Why did you like it?

9. Write a character sketch of any person of your acquaintance who reminds you of any character in a book. Try to explain the resemblances as fully and vividly as you can.

13. Tell, from the point of view of one of the chief characters, the story of some narrative poem.

When the College Board began to work on developing its new Comprehensive Examination form of the English entrance exam, it based many of its decisions on a precedent established by Harvard. As a spokesman for the National Conference on Uniform Entrance Requirements in English explained, the suggestions from that body to the College Board in 1915 culminated in a proposal that the colleges "set such a paper as, for example, the Harvard New Plan paper for 1911" (Leonard 298). Such an examination, conference members agreed, should "presuppose the reading and study of literature, but not of a prescribed list of books," and it should offer "a test in sustained composition, and in the ability to read and explain intelligently at sight a fairly long and fairly difficult passage of prose or poetry" (Leonard 298). Within a year the College Board had put the suggestions of the National Conference into practice. According to a description published by the board in 1915, the comprehensive exam was to contain questions that required candidates to be able to "apply what they have learned to the solution of unexpected problems" (Commission on English 7). The board's prescriptions, in other words, described a prototype for preparation, but modifications of that model were becoming acceptable within certain unstated parameters. "Success in the examination will not necessarily depend upon a knowledge of the subject matter of the particular books prescribed in the 'Uniform Entrance Requirements in English,'" the board went on to explain, "though no candidate who has been intelligently prepared under these requirements should find himself at any disadvantage" (Commission on English 7–8).

To a large extent the College Board's shift in emphasis from textual recall to more general reading and writing ability was a response to the complaints of secondary teachers that the early examinations' concern for specific textual detail resulted in a secondary English curriculum that, for the sake of a few students preparing for higher education, was limited to detailed study of a small number of prescribed books. When the National Conference on Uniform Entrance Requirements in English met in 1915, high school and preparatory teachers in attendance complained that in order to be effective educators they needed more freedom to design a curriculum adapted to their particular student populations. As a result of such complaints, the College Board supplemented its narrowly prescriptive reading list with an alternative second list that offered a much broader choice of "recommended" rather than required works. Both of these exams were used concurrently for nearly twenty years, though the shorter, "restricted" form quickly fell into disuse after the comprehensive list was introduced and was labled "unimportant" by the board. The essential difference between these two forms of the English examination lay in the prescriptive status of their reading lists. The original, restricted exam featured a list divided into two sections, one for reading and comprehension and one for close study (i.e., textual analysis and memorization). The reading list for the comprehensive exam, on the other hand, was far more extensive and, as the Commission on English noted, was in no way prescriptive (7). The comprehensive list, in other words, purportedly extended greater professional autonomy to secondary teachers, since it merely suggested to them works the board considered appropriate for preparatory education in English. Students and teachers were free to select some items from the list and to exclude others. Moreover, they could supplement the list with comparable readings of their own choosing.

The first thirty years of the College Board's existence, then, were marked by a diminishing concern for the candidates' abilities to memorize and recall the form and content of literary texts. Instead the board grew to value the type of writing performance in which candidates demonstrated their ability to think for themselves in free literary discussion and to apply their reading and writing experiences to the interpretation of unfamiliar literary passages.

This shift in emphasis, from mastery of factual information contained in or regarding specific literary texts to mastery of a more general ability to read even unfamiliar texts with comprehension and appreciation, registers the profession's need to define its product in more pragmatic terms than had hitherto been the case. But while the ability to negotiate unfamilar textual material might well be a useful commodity to the general public, the retention of literary source material as the means of conveying and testing that ability became a means by which the profession could preserve the esoteric nature of its knowledge base. As we shall discover, the distinction between literary and nonliterary literacy soon became the basis for establishing a hierarchy within the profession. To the extent that such a hierarchy has found expression in English studies' entrance exams, it has been used as a criterion for inclusion and exclusion—not to the realm of higher education in general, but to the particular terrain of the professional community of English studies. Movement in this direction was clearly in evidence by the 1920s, when the College Board began to divide its English exam into literary and nonliterary essay portions. Appropriately, as it turns out, nonliterary composition always appeared at the very end of the examination format.

Representative of the College Board's adaptation of the Harvard New Plan exam is the 1921 Comprehensive Examination in English, which contained the following questions:

Part I

1. (Write upon 1, and upon either 2, 3, or 4) State very briefly what you remember most clearly and vividly from each of six books that you have read. So far as you can, give in two instances the reasons for your vivid impressions.

2. A great critic has described the ideal hero of a tragedy as "a man who is just, yet whose misfortune is brought about not by vice or depravity but by some error or frailty. He must be one who is highly renowned and prosperous." With this definition in mind, discuss one of Shakespeare's heroes.

3. How does the conception of a heroic character defined in Question 2 apply to the hero of some modern tragedy you have read or seen?

4. Select an important situation in a novel which you have read. (Do not discuss any book chosen in answering Question 1.) Is the action of the leading characters in this situation consistent with their actions in the previous course of the story? Explain your answer.

Part II reproduces a passage from William James's *Talks to Teachers* and asks the following questions:

a) State, in a single sentence, the theme which is common to these two paragraphs.

b) State, in not more than two sentences, the application which is made of this common theme in the first paragraph.

c) State similarly the application made of it in the second paragraph.

The second section of part II reproduces a sonnet by Keats, "The Poetry of Earth is never Dead," and asks the following questions:

a) In what two lines has Keats made clear both the subject of the sonnet and the two parts into which it falls? What is the theme of each part?

b) In the second part of the sonnet, where does the theme of the first part reappear? In what *two* ways, then, has Keats given unity to the sonnet? What contrast of seasons lends variety to this unity?

c) With the aid of what you have now observed, summarize the sonnet in two sentences (leaving out, if you wish, the two lines which state its subject).

Part III, apparently intended to provide an indication of students' breadth of reading, lists the titles of twenty books and asks students to name the authors of five of them and to tell in three or four sentences what they know of the books.

Part IV lists fifteen topics from which students were to choose one on which to write a composition of about 400 words. Only three of the topics are related to literature (and in only the most general way), and students are instructed to adhere to the following guidelines: "Choose such aspects of the subject as you can well discuss according to an orderly, consecutive plan, in which each paragraph shall be one stage." The fifteen topics are as follows:

1. Books I have outgrown.

2. Gardens.

3. Home decoration.

4. The characteristics of the people in some section of the United States.

5. The connection between the life of some author and his work.

6. What life in the United States will probably be like in 1950.

7. What I like in present-day literature.

8. The United States and world peace.

9. The opportunity of women in politics.

10. The significance of fuel (or transportation) in the life of a modern community.

11. Food, regarded as either a scientific or an economic problem.

12. The most useful machine I know.

13. How my community (state, town, or school) is governed.

14. How to make moving pictures better.

15. Democracy in school life.

In articulating the aims it hoped to accomplish with exams of this sort, the College Board described its comprehensive examination in English for the years 1929–34 as serving a two-fold purpose. Not only would it "test powers of correct, clear, truthful expression" in the nonliterary composition section, but it would additionally "enable the candidate to show that he has understood and appreciated a sufficient amount of English literature." It was the latter category of exam question, calling for interpretation of unfamiliar literary passages, that purportedly measured "the candidate's ability to think for himself and to apply what he has learned" (Commission on English 8).

The course of the CEEB English exam's development throughout its first thirty years registers a gradual erosion of eastern college domination in the face of the pragmatic demands of the western schools. It traces a general shift in the underlying definition of academic literacy from the mastery, largely through memorization, of a select group of texts, to the more general ability to comprehend and appreciate literature and to interpret new literary works in light of previous reading experience. Such a progression clearly parallels the board's overarching interest during this time in academic aptitude rather than scholastic achievement as the measure of the individual's probable success in college. Indeed it was not long before the College Board's objective Scholastic Aptitude Test (SAT), first implemented in 1926, began to displace essay examinations in all subjects, including English, as the measure preferred by member colleges to assist in admissions decisions.

Characteristics of Entrance Testing During the Era of Belletristic Literacy

Before proceeding to a discussion of the SAT itself and the modern era of objective testing, it is worthwhile to examine some of the actual essay test questions that represent concerns and imply values held by the board—as well as by selective colleges that persevered in composing their own entrance exams—during the period when a strong belletristic bias characterized the prevailing conception of academic literacy. Collectively, the examinations of the period illustrate three general patterns of development that characterized the emerging professional identity of English studies specialists as they attempted to reconcile or somehow balance the often conflicting fields of composition and literature. First, and especially fundamental to these negotiations, is the profession's changing conceptualization of rhetoric. As the examination questions featured in this chapter reveal, the position of rhetoric within the professional knowledge base of English studies can be charted according to the ways in which exam questions build or neglect to build a rhetorical situation into the examination process. Secondly, the progression of exam questions through the early years of the profession, coupled in some cases with examiners' commentaries in response to selected exams, traces a concern for the intergrity of the literary canon and a desire to keep literary culture separate and distinct from popular culture. Finally, we can observe the introduction of nonliterary composition topics into entrance exams that otherwise focus on purely literary types of knowledge, a development that not only represented but helped to seal the division of literature and composition into two separate branches of the profession.

The Changing Face of Rhetoric

In 1874 President Eliot's expressed hope for the new "literary composition" form of the English entrance exam at Harvard was that it would serve to highlight the importance of "rhetorical correctness" in written English, by which was meant an adherence to the mechanical conventions of Standard Written English and to academically prescribed organizational patterns. To the present-day rhetorician, accustomed to perceiving rhetoric in terms of appropriateness rather than correctness, the coupling of the terms *rhetoric* and *correctness* makes for an oddly disparate combination. Indeed, the prescriptive sense of Eliot's notion of rhetoric is pointedly absent from Lloyd-Jones's considerably more recent definition of rhetoric as "the study of effective choices among linguistic and discursive alternatives." To accept such a definition, according to Lloyd-Jones, necessitates putting aside questions of correctness, since "doctrines of correctness tend to allow little room for choice because they treat variant forms as falling away from excellence" (169).

As chapter 3 has shown, Eliot's prescriptive-formalist definition of rhetoric held sway for many years in entrance examinations, with instructions emphasizing correctness in such formal systems as spelling, punctuation, capitalization, and sentence and paragraph structure. On such examinations, the few questions that explicitly addressed rhetorical concerns generally called for the identification of various tropes and figures, further emphasizing the formal and formulaic nature of rhetoric as perceived by English studies specialists. Issues of audience, purpose, and appropriate text type were essentially absent from both the questions and the instructions of such exams, which typically directed students to simply "write a brief composition" or "write an essay" on topics chosen from a list of options.

In the 1901 College Board examination, for instance, students were instructed to "write a composition, at least two or more pages of the examination book in length, correct in paragraph and sentence structure and in general arrangement on each of three subjects which you select from the following list." The majority of the topics in the list that followed might well have served as essay titles: for example, "The fifth act of *The Merchant of Venice*" or "*The Spectator* and its authors" (13).

Nondirective essay prompts such as these were the rule in early College Board English exams, although interspersed among them were prompts worded in such a way as to specify a particular rhetorical mode. Specifications of purpose and audience were uniformly absent, however. In the 1903 exam, for instance, appears the prompt, "*Compare* the mental struggle of Brutus and the conflict in Shylock's mind between avarice and the desire for revenge," (25) and in the 1904 exam students were directed, "*Explain* the speech below, stating under what circumstances it was made" (24), and "Write a brief composition, or essay, giving the substance of the opening speech of *Comus, describing* the Attendant Spirit and the enchanter, and *explaining* the part played by each in the allegory" (23) (emphasis added).

Such essay prompts were increasingly prevalent in the College Board's exams, and by 1910 they had, in fact, become the dominant form. In the "Reading and Practice" portion of the 1910 exam, the word "describe" opens eight of nineteen total questions (24–25). Two questions ask examinees to "tell" or "narrate"; three call for "discussion," and two ask that the writer "explain" or "show how" (24–25). The remaining four prompts appear as direct questions requiring a fairly specific mode of response: for example, "Did Rebecca, in *Ivanhoe,* deserve a better fate?" (25) and "What qualities of Henry Esmond cause him to be considered a noble and interesting character?" (25).

The progression toward this greater degree of rhetorical specificity in essay instructions was fairly consistent throughout the first decade of the College Board's existence, with the odd exception of 1909, when students, as in the very earliest exams, were instructed in parts I and III to "write a composition, at least two paragraphs in length, correct in paragraph and sentence structure and in general arrangement"(22) on selected topics, all of which were presented as titlelike words or phrases. Part I selections include the following:

1. Orlando in the Forest of Arden
2. The plot of King Henry the Fifth
3. Noble elements in the character of Brutus
4. Malvolio
5. The pound of flesh

Part III selections are very similar in kind:

1. The spectre of the bridegroom
2. My impression of the *Essays of Elia*
3. Joan of Arc
4. The hero as prophet
5. A summary of one of Emerson's Essays (23)

In 1908 the appearance of one particular essay option that, in effect, builds the rhetorical situation into the prompt, giving students fairly specific information about their prescribed audience, purpose, and text type, marks the beginning of a second trend toward even greater rhetorical specificity in examination instructions. In the 1908 exam, students are asked to "write a letter to a friend describing the trial scene in *The Merchant of Venice,* assuming you had just seen it on stage for the first time, and that neither of you had ever heard of the play before" (22).

In subsequent years, questions of this type appeared with increasing regularity. As the board's membership grew more and more concerned with students' ability to appreciate literature by approaching reading as an exercise of the imagination, the aesthetic and moral sensitivity, and the understanding, questions like these began to require students to enter imaginatively into the experience of particular characters within various literary works. The prescribed novels, plays, poems, and essays, then, were invoked to provide considerably detailed information about a fabricated rhetorical context for the examinees' responses. In 1911, for example, students were given two such essay options:

> Supposing yourself to be Orlando (in *As You Like It*), write a letter to someone at court, describing the people to be met in the Forest of Arden, and setting forth the advantages of woodland life over life at court. (8)

> Tell, from the point of view of the chief character, the story of one of the poems of Scott, Byron, Macaulay, Poe, Tennyson, or Browning. (9)

In 1912 and 1913 similar questions appear, asking students, for example, to "tell the story of the latter part of *Twelfth Night* from the point of view of Sebastian" (1912, 10) and to write "a brief *Spectator* paper on some person you know" (1913, 13). Such questions not only required examinees to empathize with various fictional characters and literary personages but also directed them to refer to explicitly literary models in their efforts to fictionalize a rhetorical situation, complete with audience and purpose.

As the comprehensive exam greatly reduced the authority of the prescribed reading list, however, and as nonliterary topics gradually came to be the accepted norm, "context-laden" essay prompts similarly took on a nonliterary character. The 1912 exam, for instance, contains the question, "Have you in mind any poem not read in your school which you think ought to be read there? In a letter addressed to the Principal, ask to have it added to the list of required reading, and give your reasons for the request" (16). In the following years, questions that provide information about rhetorical context continue to define a nonliterary context, requiring examinees to refer to their own everyday experiences and observations for the information needed for fictionalizing various aspects of the rhetorical situation. In the 1915 exam, for instance, the topic, "the person, scene, or incident that has most impressed you this week," is accompanied by the instructions, "Write this composition as a familiar letter" (30). And in 1918, knowledge of the student's own school rather than a literary text is required in order to build the rhetorical situation specified by the prompt, "Imagine yourself chosen by your school-mates to head a committee to lay before the principal some question of importance to the spirit or morale of the school. Write a connected and clear presentation of the issues involved, with the view of submitting it for criticism to the members of your committee" (23). Similarly, a context-laden prompt from the College Board's 1924 exam, though its subject is essentially literary, specifies a text-type and a rhetorical situation that the student can build only on the basis of familiarity with such nonliterary elements as the school newspaper textual format and an audience of student readers: "Write for your school paper a review of a modern play, or of an anthology of recent poetry, or of a modern novel" (18).

In the first twenty-five years of the College Board exams then can be traced a number of important developments in English studies' consideration of rhetoric and its place in the literacy instruction of high school and college students. Originally perceived as primarily a matter of formal correctness, rhetoric, in accordance with the pragmatic interests of a growing number of state, western, and vocationally oriented CEEB members, eventually acquired certain aspects of the currently endorsed definition of communicative choices based on purposeful intent and social context. The early stages of that development were marked by a reliance upon literary texts to provide the rhetorical elements of purpose, social context, and even ethos. Subsequent developments in standardized entrance exams, however, served to focus attention on students' abilities to communicate effectively in situations similar to those they would conceivably experience in their own lives. Along with the trend toward greater specificity of rhetorical situation came an increasing emphasis on persuasive discourse as opposed to the virtual exclusiveness of the very early College Board exams' concern for descriptive and narrative compositions.

Finally, it appears that the increasing emphasis of the exams on the production of purposeful, and especially persuasive, written texts and on more naturalistic as opposed to purely literary contexts corresponds in the main with a general trend in American education during the early twentieth century—namely, a growing tendency to reject elitist definitions of higher education as something befitting only the leisure class. As the academy opened its doors wider to admit the working class and other nontraditional students, its standards of literacy changed to correspond with the more practical concerns and needs of the new student population. Accordingly, we find that the prescriptive formalism of an early academic understanding of the rhetoric of written language gradually gave way to a more pragmatic conception that began to resemble the notion of rhetoric that has recently started to flourish in connection with composition studies. Interestingly, the changing concept of rhetoric reflected by standardized entrance exams continued to be viewed through the lens of literature during the early years of the twentieth century, an inevitable result of the powerful influence of academic literacy's origins in the textual study of the classical canon.

Concern for the Integrity of the Canon

By its very nature, the literary construction of literacy recorded in English entrance exams of the late nineteenth and early twentieth centuries required a familiarity with and a respect for the works constituting the English literary canon. Examination questions during that time asked students to demonstrate their knowledge of the content of certain privileged texts and to prove their mastery of the accepted conventions of literary language use as well as their breadth of literary reading. Two major developments in standardized college entrance exams during the second decade of the twentieth century, however, appear to mark the ending of an era in which the literary canon represented the single collection of texts to be used as measures of academic literacy. In 1911, following an example set by a number of colleges that independently administered their own entrance exams, the College Board began offering nonliterary topics as options in the extended composition section of the exam. And in 1916, the board administered its first comprehensive English examination, a development that no longer limited exam questions to topics suggested by a prescribed set of works representing the canon. Instead, comprehensive examinations took into account a variable and indefinite collection of works students might encounter in reading directed either by their secondary teachers or by their own interests and inclinations.

But while both of these developments in the College Board's exam might well be taken as evidence that the literary canon was losing its supremacy as an academic standard of literate accomplishment, other evidence suggests that in actual practice, evaluators continued to assess student performance on the exam according to standards that effectively safeguarded the integrity of the canon.

In 1930, the College Board formed the Commission on English to study the entrance examination in English and to report its findings regarding the exam's validity and its reception among participating institutions. As part of its study, the commission reviewed a random sampling of graded comprehensive examination papers from 1929, dividing them according to the scores—ranging from 25 to 95—that they had received from the original scorers. The commission's written report to the board selects from its sampling of papers individual examinations that received scores of 50, 55, 60, and so on, up to 95 and reproduces them, along with the examiners' comments. Of particular interest is the sample paper scored 50, a score that, according to the commission, indicates among other failings a "deficiency in reading" (50).

In the commission's study, the examination book scored 50 received only two brief comments from the original examiners: "deficient in reading" and "paragraphing defective," and it is the former that the commission chose for elaboration in a commentary opening with the claim, "This paper fails because the candidate has shown no real acquaintance with standard literature" (60). Most disturbing to both the original examiners and the commission members seems to have been the student's essay response to the following prompt:

> A critic has said that the reader may have these attitudes toward his reading:
>
> (a) He may be interested primarily in incidents.
>
> (b) He may share in the emotions and thoughts of the characters in critical moments.

Illustrate these statements, using specific illustrations from your reading of four works, representing at least two different types of literature. (56)

In responding to this question, the student whose paper merited the score of 50 centers his discussion on *Quentin Durwood, Beau Geste,* and two contemporary novels, *The Day the World Ended,* by Sax Rohmer, and *The Nervous Wreck,* a work of unspecified authorship. This unfortunate choice of readings, according to the commission's report, is justifiable cause for the student's failure. No doubt the student helped to seal his own fate with his favorable comment about modern adventure and mystery novels in his final composition on the topic "My Literary Bypaths": "Many modern novels are of course written for moral purposes, and many of them are adventure novels, or mysteries. These types please me" (59). The commission's summary comment on the exam concludes that the student's interest is in "stories which are trivial and sensational" at the expense of "standard literature":

> This paper fails because the candidate has shown no real acquaintance with standard literature. He refers to *Quentin Durward* with a slight reference and mentions two poems of Wordsworth. He shows that his chief interest, however, is in stories which are trivial and sensational.
> Moreover he has no power even of adequate reproduction. Whatever the study of literature may have done for him, there is no evidence here that it has formed his taste or has given him even slight reflective power. (60)

Further discussion by the commission reveals that such deficiencies in reading were by no means limited to that particular college applicant. Indeed, one of the most frequently voiced criticisms of the comprehensive examination was the complaint that by relaxing the prescriptive nature of the reading list, the exam "did not guard against the use of ephemeral modern novels" (113). Elsewhere in its report, the commission reiterates the same criticism itself, noting that a considerable threat undermining the purposes of the Comprehensive Examination in English comes from the possible introduction of modern popular works to the student's literary preparation—works whose quality has not been submitted to the test of time: "In individual papers and individual questions [the exams] have been insufficiently comprehensive, allowing too narrow a range of reading, particularly of inferior contemporary literature" (125).

Criticisms such as these prompted the commission's recommendation that the board should more sharply define its evaluation criteria by publishing a definition of "good literature" (50). To be sure, some notion of how "good" and "bad" literature should be differentiated seems to have been important to the examiners throughout the first thirty years of the board's operation. The commission's description of comprehensive books receiving a score of less than 50 opens with the observation that the writers of the books typically reveal promiscuous reading habits.

Throughout its history the board seems to have demonstrated a consistent desire to preserve the integrity of the canon, not only by penalizing students for discussing nonstandard works but also by phrasing examination questions in such a way as to mandate a positive response to specific works in the canon, based on descriptions of those works as interesting, vivid, attractive, appealing, intriguing, beautiful, admirable, enriching, or immortal. The following examples, drawn from College Board examinations between 1902 and 1926, are representative of such essay prompts:

> How does the use of contrast in the character and setting add to the interest of *The Merchant of Venice?* (1902, 21)
>
> What are the most striking poetic characteristics of the *Ancient Mariner?* (1902, 21)
>
> If Boswell "could not reason, had no wit, no humour, and no eloquence," why is it that his "writings are likely to be read as long as English exists, either as a dead or a living language"? (1908, 24)
>
> Narrate what was to you the most interesting incident in one of the novels among the prescribed books. (1909, 22)
>
> Discuss the chief merits of Macaulay's style. (1910, 27)
>
> Identify the poetry passage (reproduced on the examination form) and discuss it in terms of its main thought, its subject matter, and its "poetic beauty." (1910, 24)
>
> Describe the scene which most strongly appealed to you in

one of the following novels: *Quentin Durward, Ivanhoe, Silas Marner,* or *Lorna Doone* (1911, 9)

What images, or pictures, in *The Ancient Mariner* do you remember most vividly? (1912, 11)

Which of the shorter poems in the *Golden Treasury* do you most admire, and for what reasons? (1913, 13)

For what qualities other than its humor do you find one of Shakespeare's comedies attractive? (1915, 32)

In what ways have the stories which you have read in preparation for this examination enlarged *either* your knowledge of human life lying outside your own experience *or* your ideas of how a story should be told? (1915, 32)

Why do you think poetry is not more read nowadays? What lyric poet do you think most likely to appeal to persons of your acquaintance not now interested in poetry? On what grounds do you recommend this poet? (1915, 32)

Explain specifically what you have gained from reading (a) a novel (b) a drama (c) a group of essays (or an oration) (d) a biography (or a narrative poem). (1924, 22)

"The memory of Johnson keeps many of his works alive." What was it about Johnson that keeps his works alive? (1924, 19)

Which one of the authors (other than Shakespeare) whose works you have read during the past year should you like to know better? What specific qualities of this author's work have produced this desire in you? (1926, 32)

Regarding the final example, an examination reader from Yale is reported to have made the comment, "It is possible for a candidate not to desire further the acquaintance of any author read during the period. This being the case, he is compelled either to 'fill' the question or to become exceedingly disingenuous" (Commission on English, 136). The Commission on English accepted the validity of this comment, and in doing so it seemed to acknowledge the discipline's obligation to provide a service at least partially defined by the standards of nonprofessionals. In making the student's own interest and "common sense" more important criteria than professionally devised standards of literate performance, the commission's official statement indirectly espoused the philosophy of literacy for life over literacy for school.

> Such criticisms cannot be disposed of as mere moral over-nicities. If the student, to answer a question in what his common sense tells him is an adequate way, must invent feelings that he thinks he ought to have about literature, or compose something that he thinks an essay is supposed to be, instead of writing something that he is interested in saying, he will not give evidence of his actual ability. (137)

Very infrequently the College Board examinations featured questions that invited students to respond either positively or negatively to works on the list; by far the dominant means of prompting students to demonstrate their powers of literary criticism and appreciation was with questions that assumed their positive responses to standard works of literature. This has been true not only in the English entrance examination's development under the auspices of the College Board but also in a good many examinations administered independently by various university English departments both prior to and concurrent with administration of the College Board's exams.

The endurance of the tendency to slant questions requiring critical or appreciative responses, despite developments in admissions testing that apparently undermined the authority of the canon to set standards for academic literacy, testifies to the virulence of literature-based literacy in English studies departments. The Commission on English, in the same document in which they apparently supported the validity of the examinee's "common sense," concluded that applicants who clearly failed the College Board's entrance exam in English, thereby demonstrating their unfitness for higher education, failed because they were unable to respond positively to the language and the ideas presented in literary works. In short, they were unable or unwilling to allow literary experience to articulate their own life experience; their lives were too out-of-step with life as it appeared in the pages of great literature:

> The important thing is that reading for themselves has not been a genuine experience. The symbols on the printed page have not been fused by imaginative understanding into their minds. This failure to make the transfer from the symbols

to the real experience is proved by the regular failure of these books in Part II. These students can read and understand words, but they cannot grasp meanings as wholes when one must understand words combined into phrases and the images and ideas which the phrases express. The study of literature for them is apparently something apart from real life, something arbitrary and conventional, to be mastered for an examination. At their best they merely absorb what they read; they do not reflect upon it and make it part of their own mental equipment. (48)

The concept of literacy implied by such a commentary coincides with what Szwed in 1981 described as an "outdated model of literacy inherited from 19th-century, upper-class Europe." Such a model includes the belief that "book life" is "somehow greater than real life" and therefore provides an avenue of transcendence. A further characteristic of this literacy model, according to Szwed, is its implicit mistrust of mass culture and of the masses themselves. In particular, it rejects the appeal of universal education, on the premise that educating the masses necessarily involves a "cheapening or a debasing of culture, language, and literature" (18).

Viewed as a means of defining and retaining control of the expertise that constitutes a professional knowledge base, the literacy model assailed by Szwed became, in the hands of English studies specialists, an effort to articulate the kind of talent or charismatic knowledge that is not subject to instruction and is therefore exempt from standardization. Such knowledge, as Larson tells us, is highly regarded within the professional community itself, and because to possess it requires special gifts, acknowledging the existence of that sort of talent is crucial to a profession's autonomy. Ironically, then, the project of standardizing literacy in academic form necessitates some acceptance of the claim that literacy is a matter of inborn ability. A particularly forceful spokesman for that premise was M. L. Crossley of Wesleyan University, whose report on factors contributing to poor work in college included the claim that illiteracy was inherited:

> Each year the number of men entering college with the handicap of family illiteracy grows larger and the problems which they create in education become increasingly complex. These men and their parents are chips off the same

blocks and their intellectual inheritances from the race largely determine what they will accomplish in the pursuit of an education. (952)

The entrance examinations of the College Board began to acknowledge the influence of the "inheritance factor" during the late 1920s when English exams began to differentiate between the literary and nonliterary student. The board's approach was to divide students into two camps within the academic community and, in subtle ways, to privilege one group over the other. On the one hand there were those students whose natural inclination was toward literary studies, and on the other there were those whose aptitude was for science and technology.

Consideration of the two groups was first applied with explicit intent to the formulation of Restricted Examination questions, which continued to be drawn from works on a prescribed reading list. During the late 1920s, according to the historical survey of College Board English exams conducted by the Commission on English in 1931, the board made "an apparently careful attempt so to arrange questions as to make it possible for the non-literary student to pass the examination by paraphrase, reproduction, and exact memory of the major classics" (5–6). The literary students, on the other hand, were provided with opportunities to select questions that allowed them to "show [their] powers" as these applied to the prescribed reading (6).

Likewise, with respect to the Comprehensive Examination in English, the commission's 1931 report recommended that the range of questions be expanded to recognize and provide opportunities to both "the candidate who possesses superior powers" and "the non-literary candidate who will require English as an instrument to be used in technical courses or in other than purely English studies" (125). In a subsequent portion of its report, the commission clarified its rationale for the recommendation, characterizing literary students as those who are more imaginative, less bound by the mundanities of real-life experience than their more vocationally oriented companions:

> English teachers are perhaps likely to show an unconscious preference for the literary theme. The Commission therefore wishes to commend the examiners for the policy of includ-

ing in the list of theme topics titles which the scientific or literal minded student would naturally welcome. A student entering an institution that lays its chief emphasis upon mechanical or engineering courses needs high efficiency in English, but it is of a different type of efficiency. He needs this ability for effective handling, logical development, and careful organization of facts. He should aim for substance and precision. The list of topics would, of course, offer equal opportunity for the student of the opposite type—the student of romantic temperament who delights in giving his fancy free rein. The list, indeed, should be so full and varied that each student may find among the offering something appropriate to his temperament and training. (217)

According to this examination formula, the populist philosophy of education for life is expanded by a twofold definition of *life*. Not only does the term encompass a utilitarian, vocational perspective on human existence, but it includes as well an antivocational perspective that finds human purpose embodied in literary texts. Education for life and education for more education in the classical sense are thereby joined into a single concept of higher education, but within that single concept they continue to be hierarchically arranged. By formulating a twofold definition of their professional product as one that satisfies utilitarian demands and at the same time provides a pathway for rising above such demands, English studies yielded to the scientific ideal of efficiency while at the same time preserving its identity within the liberal arts tradition.

It is significant that both the College Board and the Commission on English designated only the composition section of the exam as the proper place for recognizing different temperaments and disciplinary aptitudes among college applicants. Reading portions of the exam continued to be strictly literary. In 1931, when the commission issued its report, the Comprehensive Examination consisted of three parts: part I was designed to test the student's literary background; part II called for "accurate reading of poetry or of poetry and prose"; and part III contained a list of topics from which the candidate was to select one as the subject for a composition or theme. Throughout the history of the Comprehensive Examination, only part III was ever affected by the board's concern for the nonliterary student, while the reading sections reflected the importance of literary study as the special province of the discipline. As the commission's report acknowledged, many courses other than English shared the aim of teaching students to translate text into perception, but English alone shouldered the responsibility of sharpening students' sensitivities to the aesthetics of language and opening them to the imaginative realms of literature. This, then, was the exclusive domain for the development of highly specialized professional knowledge and the expression of talent:

> [English teachers] are almost alone responsible for showing the student something about the facts and forms of literature, the principles of thought communication through language, and what it means to read imaginative material, fiction, drama, and poetry. It is through his English courses that a student must learn what the content of such imaginative literature is: the pictures it may paint of the world of nature and the world of man; the ideas, moods, aspirations, struggles, that it may express; the beauty of melody and form that it may convey. (184)

During the first thirty years of the twentieth century, as secondary and college student populations expanded to include an increasing diversity of students who held varying notions about the purposes of education, the definition of literacy basics as recorded in English entrance examinations necessarily underwent radical transformations. To meet the demands of students whose interests and goals lay well outside the provisions of a liberal arts education rooted in the classical tradition, English studies acknowledged the practical need to cultivate nonliterary language use in composition courses implementing a vocationally oriented slant on the education-for-life philosophy. But while the discipline was relatively willing to accept the validity of nonliterary texts in its writing instruction, reading, as it figured in the instructional curriculum of English studies, retained a predominantly literary character. In large part, this particular step in the division of literature and composition seems to have been motivated by a concern that, in the increasing pragmatism of the high school and college curriculum, the traditional humanistic values of textual studies would be lost were personnel in the department of

English not willing to serve as guardians of high culture through the study of exclusively literary texts.

The Divorce of Literary Subject Matter and Student Composition

Among the innovations that the 1911 Harvard New Plan exam introduced to the College Board was the use of composition topics drawn from students' own probable experience and from academic subjects such as history and science, in addition to English or American literature. In the September 1911 exam at Harvard, for instance, the following options comprised the list of composition topics for "Section B," a section requiring a composition of some length that would enable students to demonstrate their abilities to "make one point grow naturally into the other and to fit one paragraph firmly and neatly onto the other" (Greenough 373):

7. Any one of the questions under [Section] A [all literary topics] that you have not already answered.
8. A description of some person, house, or village with which you are familiar.
9. Write a short account of the career and aims of some *one* of the following persons: Aeneas, Pericles, Charlemagne, Cromwell, Alexander Hamilton.
10. Which of your studies do you think has done you the most good? Why?
11. Photographic plates.
12. Wireless telegraphy. (Greenough 371)

The practice of offering composition topics of a nonliterary nature entered College Board policy directly via the influence of Harvard, but Harvard was certainly not the first institution to approve such a practice. As we have already seen, non–Ivy League colleges such as Stanford, the University of Texas, and the Free Academy of New York were already using a nonliterary approach to testing composition skills in the late nineteenth century. And even among the prestigious endowed schools, Harvard could look to a precedent in that policy. As early as 1908, according to the report of the Committee on Entrance Requirements to the New England Association of Teachers of English, the Massachusetts Institute of Technology "threw over altogether" its list of required literary readings and adopted in its place a requirement of "work in composition on non-literary subjects, with 'sight questions' to test a student's power of understanding and appreciating literature" (New England Association 654).

Nonliterary composition topics were first introduced into the College Board's English exams in 1911, the same year they were first used at Harvard. Like the Harvard examiners, the board attempted to draw topics from academic subjects such as history and science as well as from the students' own probable experiences or observations. Of the ten options for composition topics in part II of the College Board's 1911 exam, four require some knowledge of specific works on the prescribed reading list, one requires reference to reading the student may have done outside of the reading list (one question calls for a composition on "good points of my favorite novel"), and the remaining five require no literary reading at all:

6. Some influences of Magna Carta upon English history.

7. The causes of the American Civil War.

8. My reasons for going to college.

9. Characteristics of the people, or of the scenery, in some locality with which I am familiar (the exact title to be chosen by the candidate).

10. Characteristic traits of some bird, fish, or other animal (exact title to be chosen by the candidate). (19)

In 1912, only four of the ten composition topics offered were directed toward prescribed readings; the remaining six covered areas such as sports, history, and personal observation and experience (21). By 1913, none of the composition topics required discussion of the content of prescribed readings, and only two asked for biographical knowledge of specific authors (topic 9 is "How Shakespeare became a successful playwright," and topic 10 asks about "Milton's service to his country and the relation of this activity to his literary career") (23). Introduced in the 1913 exam are topics drawn from current events and contemporary life; for instance, prompt 1 asks for a discussion of "some aspects of the last presidential campaign," and prompt 6 asks for the applicant's views on "the moral and educational influence of moving-picture shows" (23).

In succeeding years, although an occasional literary topic cropped up from time to time, nonliterary topics continued to be the rule in the composition section of the College Board's English exam, a condition coinciding with the official division of the exam in 1915 into two separate parts: "Grammar and Composition" and "Literature." After this split, the literature section was limited to prompts of the type already illustrated above, while the grammar and composition section was gradually set free from literary texts altogether. Compare, for example, the grammar question included in the study and practice section of the 1902 exam with those which constituted the grammar and composition section of the 1915 exam:

1902

"She is the hopeful lady of my earth:
But woo her, gentle Paris, get her heart;
My will to her consent is *but* a part;
An she agree within her scope of choice
Lies my consent and fair according voice."

"And, Nevil, this I do assure myself:
Richard shall live to make the Earl of Warwick
The greatest man in England *but* the King."

Explain fully the three different uses of *but* in the passages here quoted, noting in each case the grammatical relations of the principal and subordinate clauses in the first passage quoted. (22)

1915

I. a) Explain the grammatical relation of each clause in the following sentence:

I do not know why so much that is hard is interwoven in our life here; but I see that it is meant to be so interwoven.

I. b) Copy the following sentences, making such changes as you think necessary:

Between you and I, I think I would prefer not to publicly acknowledge the mistake.

Each one said good-bye in their own way.

Tell me all the circumstances, both pleasant and otherwise.

Those roses may smell as sweetly as you say, but it don't
matter to me, for I've got an awful cold. (30)

The division between composition and literature accomplished
through developments in the College Board's English entrance examination up to this point paved the way toward an eventual distinction
between aptitude and achievement in English studies. With the introduction of the SAT in 1926, grammar and composition was firmly
established in the realm of college admissions testing as a "content-
free" skill (and thus, an aptitude rather than an achievement), no
longer tied to literature as it had been in the late nineteenth and
early twentieth centuries. Literature, on the other hand, came to be
recognized as an independent subject, the mastery of which was
labeled a scholastic achievement, subject to assessment only in the
board's series of achievement tests administered apart from the SAT.

Interestingly, however, as the SAT's objective and indirect format
for testing literacy skills precluded any actual composition on the part
of students taking the examination, the achievement test in literature
and language became the only type of entrance exam offered by the
College Board that called for actual composition as well as sustained
reading. In practice then, and almost by default, composition and
literature were essentially reunited in the College Board's achievement
exams when the SAT rose to prominence. After verbal aptitude came
to be recognized as a measure of probable success in English studies
and related fields, however, both literature and composition began
to suffer a loss of status among designated entrance subjects. This
development in turn challenged the profession to redefine its product
in such a way that it could survive in the competitive market with
more conspicuously utilitarian courses of study. The stakes increased
as more and more schools began to require the SAT, which measures
verbal aptitude, and to view achievement tests such as the one in
language and literature as optional or unrequired.

Chapters 5 and 6 trace the growing popularity of the SAT for
measuring academic literacy skills and examine the impact this widespread use of an objective standardized exam has had on the professional identity of English studies. Effects such as the objective testing
phenomenon has had on academic fields in general are especially
critical in the particular case of English studies, precisely because

of English studies' direct responsibility for the academy's "essential product," academic literacy. In a very concrete sense, the new objective exams, requiring little or no actual writing and a miniumum of sustained reading, called into question the presumed centrality of literacy, as it was defined by departments of English, to the academic enterprise. As objective aptitude tests became increasingly valued for their capacity to process quickly and economically the burgeoning numbers of Americans flocking to college, the age-old practice of teaching to the test was bound to have transformative consequences for American education. The political and economic rationales behind these transformations and their immediate and long-term effects upon the profession of English studies are subjects I explore in chapters 5 and 6.

CHAPTER FIVE

Objective Tests and the Construction of Literacy as Scholastic Aptitude

The professional inclination of English studies to construct literacy in terms of aptitude rather than achievement was conspicuously signaled by the introduction of the Comprehensive Examination in English in 1916, and the continuing force of that inclination is marked by the immediate popularity of that form of the exam while the older, restricted form dwindled into relative obscurity. As we have seen, the early notions of aptitude in the field of English studies were colored by the profession's heavy emphasis on literary texts. An aptitude for "high literacy"—meaning an imaginative ability to enter into the symbolic worlds constructed by written language—constituted the pinnacle of professional knowledge-making skill and was the province of only a talented few. Today, Myron Tuman assures us that the ability to construct and contemplate symbolic realities is fundamental to *all* literate activity, not just the reading and writing of literary texts. But as English entrance exams from the first twenty-five years of the College Board's existence suggest, the elevation of literary texts to a privileged realm that only the specially gifted could enter was essential to the construction of a unique professional product that could survive in a competitive market.

At the same time, however, public demand for literacy as a technology that could be employed in accomplishing social and material goals made it expedient for the profession to produce, as well, a more pedestrian version of its product. That instrumental view of literacy was advanced most forcefully by state universities, vocational schools, and research institutions founded primarily for the advancement of science and technology. In response to those influences, departments of English, which were initially established on the premises of liberal education, almost universally developed a two-part structure. On the one hand, there was the composition branch, whereby the profession discharged its most immediate service obligation to the community, and on the other hand, there was literary studies, whereby the profession maintained its special status as a guardian of culture.

For some time the use of literary works as the exclusive source of composition topics on standardized entrance exams indicated the profession's apparent desire to unify the two eventually divergent streams of expertise. While reading was featured as a means of gaining knowledge of cultural values, writing functioned as a way of demonstrating one's participation in the culture that espoused those values. Such participation necessarily extended beyond a simple knowledge of textual form; as cultural artifacts, literary works were no longer to be assimilated by memorization alone, but through the development of a sensitivity to the aesthetic properties and philosophical import of literary works in general. Educators generally concurred that such sensitivity—or "appreciation," as the examiners were more apt to label it—could be neither taught nor learned through traditional methods of memorization, drill, and "reproduction"—the written equivalent of recitation. Such traditional pedagogy, as well as the type of examinations it entailed, reflected an academic interest in literacy skills that could be measured as the individual's *achievement* in mastering a delimited body of concrete, factual knowledge. Literary appreciation, on the other hand, exceeded the boundaries of achievement in English studies, for truly appreciative students possessed special knowledge-acquisition skills enabling them to comprehend the cultural significance even of works that had not been specifically taught in the classroom. The term *aptitude* was eventually adopted to distinguish knowledge-acquisition skills—or, to use Nystrand's term, "knowing how"— from specific content knowledge—"knowing what."

The terms *aptitude* and *achievement* certainly did not originate in the discipline of English studies, nor were they used only to describe the types of procedural and content knowledge that were coming to be recognized in that field. Indeed, the concept of academic, or scholastic, aptitude had its roots in the study of psychology, particularly educational psychology, a disciplinary branch within the modern curriculum that eagerly embraced the new science of statistics in the early twentieth century.

As Applebee (1974) has observed, attempts to measure "intelligence"—a broader, more general construct than "knowledge" or "mastery" in particular subject areas—received widespread interest in this country when the Binet scales were produced between 1905 and 1908 and revised by Lewis M. Terman's Stanford revision in 1916 (*Tradition* 81). Binet himself was among the first to use aptitude in conjunction with the psychological construct of intelligence. In 1909 he wrote regarding his intentions for the intelligence scales he had developed for use with school children that he hoped to be able to identify "aptitudes" of individual children so that school programs could be adapted to their individual needs. Objecting to the educational practice of subjecting students whose intelligence differed in any way from "normal" to "a kind of instruction that was contrary to their intellectual type," Binet wrote, "It is according to children's aptitudes that they should be directed toward a profession. . . . In schools with large enrollments a method of sectioning pupils on the basis of their aptitudes would be possible" (Watson 361).

During the First World War those scales were put to use by the United States military, which found them a useful means for sorting recruits according to their abilities to perform in various positions. Once the early intelligence tests had proven successful in predicting an individual's aptitude for performing certain functions, the academic community began to express an interest in finding out whether similar tests could also predict an individual's success or failure in academic performance (see Applebee, *Tradition* 81–82). In large part this interest was prompted by huge increases in America's college-going population in the years following the First World War. Writing for the College Board in 1957, Jorgenson chronicles the increase in college attendance throughout the first half of the twentieth century with reports that in 1900 only 4 percent of the American population attended college; by 1940 the number had risen to 15 percent, and by 1954 it had risen even further, to 30 percent (xii).

For the first time in history, college campuses after World War I were faced with more applicants than existing faculty and facilities could accommodate. Colleges across the country were forced to implement selective admissions procedures to an unprecedented degree, and the trend extended even to some state universities that had established themselves upon the ideal of public access to higher education solely on the basis of successful completion of secondary schooling. Writing in 1936, R. L. Duffus described the situation:

The weaker and poorer institutions, as always, competed among themselves for students, and offered inducements of various kinds, including a degree of scholastic leniency. There was a booming market throughout the period for that singular product of higher learning, the "amateur" college athlete. The stronger institutions did come to feel, however, that they could pick and choose among those applicants who held secondary school diplomas and who were not unusually fleet of foot or strong of muscle. Even the state universities foresaw the time when they could not take in all of the nominally qualified candidates who offered themselves. There was a prospect that the quality of the student body could be improved by a judicious system of selection. (83)

To the problem of establishing selective admissions standards, the recently developed IQ tests offered a convenient solution. For some years the new science of psychometrics had been gaining recognition as a branch of study within the academic curriculum, its growth nurtured to a considerable degree by the apparent compatibility of its product with the corporate ideals of standardization and efficiency. As enrollments expanded, the college entry level became a logical focal point for academic interest in IQ, or aptitude testing. Typical of investigations into the potential value of such testing for entrance examination purposes was that of Proctor and Ward, who conducted a longitudinal study on a group of high school students in order to discover correlations between the students' general intelligence scores and their persistence in carrying out their stated plans for vocations or continued education. Four years after obtaining the intelligence test scores, Proctor and Ward reported that 81 percent of the students who undertook continued education were following through with their originally stated plans, whereas only 40 percent of those who had chosen not to pursue higher education were carrying out their stated occupational intentions. Among their conclusions to the study, Proctor and Ward claimed that "there appears to be a closer relation between intelligence and persistence in educational plans than between intelligence and persistence in vocational plans" (288) and that the median intelligence quotients of individuals who chose to continue their education were significantly higher than those of individuals choosing to work immediately after high school. As a result of their findings Proctor and Ward concluded that "measurements of general intelligence may be of great value to the vocational and educational counselor in his work" (288).

The results of Proctor and Ward's experiment raise suspicions that not only were tests useful in determining which students were likely to succeed academically, they were actually designed solely for that purpose. From the very beginning, it seems, IQ was constructed to accord with the academic community's ideas of success and self-worth. Leading to their conclusion that IQ tests could assist authorities in sorting out the appropriate vocations for young people, Proctor and Ward's study demonstrated that individuals with higher general intelligence scores were not only more likely to seek higher education, but they were also more likely to persist in the educational plans they had made than were individuals with low intelligence scores. Moreover, more intelligent high school students, they reported, typically aspired to more prestigious educational institutions and, once admitted, were likely to successfully complete their chosen courses of study within those institutions. And finally, they reported that the average intelligence test scores of students who followed academic plans that were the same as or higher than their originally stated intentions were decidedly higher than the scores of students who failed to follow through with continuing educational plans at all or who perhaps completed their continued education in lower-ranked institutions (e.g., trade schools). In the lowest-scoring group (IQ = 80–99), 63 percent persisted or improved upon their originally stated educational plans; in the middle group (IQ = 100–119), the percentage rose to 81 percent; and in the highest-scoring group (IQ = 120 or over), the percentage rose even higher, to 93 percent (286).

In 1921, the same year that Proctor and Ward's study appeared, Thorndike reported on the success of Columbia University's experiment with the actual use of an objective-type "mental test" as a part of its "new plan" of admission. Under this plan, certain applicants to Columbia College were permitted to substitute a mental test for the entrance examinations traditionally required for admission—that is, College Board exams, or in certain cases, examinations administered by the New York State Department of Education. The tests, devised by Thorndike himself, were described as "tests of mental alertness and power such as have for years been developing in psychological laboratories" ("Standard Tests for College Admission"). Thorndike had evidently adapted the principles of existing intelligence tests to the purpose of college entrance examinations by basing his questions on "an analysis of activities that the subjects are later to be required to do" ("New Plan" 95).

After reviewing the operation and success of the new plan during its first year, Thorndike was able to present evidence of the sort he hoped would make it possible "to determine with scientific accuracy whether or not the mental test is a useful addition to our academic machinery" (95). Citing a study conducted by his colleague, Ben D. Wood, of Columbia's Department of Psychology, Thorndike reports on a preliminary comparison of the relative success of four measures used to predict college performance at Columbia: the high school record, the College Board entrance examination scores, the New York Regents' examination scores, and the scores from the Thorndike psychological exam:

> The results are significant. Among the students admitted by the college entrance examinations a good many doubtful cases were included. The correlation between their examinations and their college records was +0.43 which is reasonably satisfactory. The correlation between school record and college record was +0.45. Those entering by regents' examinations were very carefully selected. The correlation between their examinations and their college records was +0.57, while the correlation between psychological examination and college record was +0.59, a highly satisfactory result. This was for the first half-year only.
>
> A similar study for the work of the whole year shows a correlation between mental test and college record of +0.60 which was remarkably good. (100-101)

(For an additional study of Thorndike intelligence examination scores as predictors of success at the Carnegie Institute, see Cleeton.)

In April of 1926, in the wake of studies such as Thorndike's and Proctor and Ward's, the College Entrance Examination Board, already an organization of national influence, offered its first Scholastic Aptitude Test (SAT) along with its standard battery of achievement tests. The creation of College Board psychometricians Carl Brigham and Cecil Brolyer, the SAT was modeled after a number of early IQ tests, among them those of Thorndike, Binet, and Terman. Because it required only short-answer responses to mostly multiple-choice questions, the SAT fell into the category of "new-type," or "objective," examinations. It is important to note that the SAT and other new-type exams originally received the label "objective" not because they were value-free in their conception, nor because the material they sought to test qualified them as neutral or disinterested measures of intellectual ability or potential, but because they required no value judgment on the part of scorers. Obviously a test of that sort was much more cost- and time-efficient to process than were the essay tests that had thus far predominated in schools and testing agencies alike. These advantages contributed to the growing popularity of the SAT among the College Board's member institutions whose governing boards, it must be recalled, were increasingly made up of financiers and corporate executives. The success of the SAT, in turn, led to the board's development in 1935 of "objective-type" achievement tests. Initially these were used only in making scholarship decisions (Bowles 14), but in 1937 the essay achievement tests administered for college entrance purposes during the April session were changed to objective-type exams (Donlan 3).

At the time, the College Board administered its entrance exams during three sessions: one in April, another in June, and another in September. Of these three, the April and June sessions were by far the most important for processing prospective college students. By 1940, the board noted that the number of applicants taking the exams in April (the session that made use of the SAT and objective achievement exams) far exceeded the number of applicants taking the exams in June. This development coincided the following year with a mutual decision by administrators at Harvard, Princeton, and Yale to initiate an accelerated wartime schedule requiring students to begin their studies in June or July rather than in September. Accordingly, in 1942, applicants to those colleges were obliged to take the April exams (Fuess 157; Donlan 3). The College Board, in turn, adapted itself to the adjusted schedule of the top Ivy League colleges, and in

1942 it abandoned the June examinations altogether, bringing to an end the era of essay-type achievement tests administered by the board.

Entrance Exams as a Means of Reconciling Professional Identity with National Interests

For most of the first half of the twentieth century, the influence of College Board tests and policies did not extend universally to all—or even to a majority of—American schools and colleges. In fact, by the end of World War II, because of widespread implementation of the high school certification plan among public schools and state universities, especially in the western and midwestern portions of the United States, the ratio of College Board member institutions to nonmembers was about one to four. In 1960, chairman of the College Board Frank Bowles calculated that by 1947 about 80 percent of all college students entered higher education through the accreditation system in which entrance examinations played an extremely minor role. The remaining 20 percent of the nation's college applicants, according to Bowles, applied to their chosen college shortly before high school graduation. A student's application materials, consequently, consisted of a high school recommendation, an incomplete school record, possibly a college official's impressions of the candidate resulting from an interview, and scores from College Board examinations taken in April or May (Bowles 10).

Within the next dozen years, however, the ratio that described the relative popularity of the two admissions systems had entirely reversed itself, and by 1960, an estimated 80 percent of all U.S. college applicants were required to take some form of examination, either the entrance examinations designed and administered at the colleges themselves or those administered by state agencies or national testing agencies such as the College Entrance Examination Board. By that time, too, the vast majority of college applicants submitted their applications before graduating from high school (Bowles 11).

The College Board, during the midtwentieth century, then, was a testing agency whose influence was rapidly gaining nationwide importance. As director Frank Bowles announced in 1948, its policies were coming to represent the colleges of the entire nation, and the board could no longer be looked upon as just a mouthpiece of the eastern colleges: "The entire country is gradually becoming the Board's stage. Although the membership is still predominantly eastern, the steady and rapid addition of colleges from the Middle West, South, and Far West augurs a day not far off when the Board will be truly representative of the entire country" (qtd. in Fuess 193).

On the one hand, then, the College Board's direct influence described in this chapter was reaching more and more institutions across the country. On the other hand, it cannot be said that the trends indicated by these policies necessarily originated with the College Board itself. Quite the contrary, with its increasing emphasis, during the first half of the twentieth century, on scholastic aptitude rather than educational achievement and on objective, or new-type, tests in place of essay examinations, the College Board was in fact responding to certain changes in the American academy, themselves symptomatic of transformations that had taken hold of American society overall. As the College Board's Commission on Tests (1974) has argued, the board, because of the widespread use of its entrance and placement tests, has in recent years come to provide a fairly accurate gauge to developments in the college admissions process as it generally exists throughout the nation:

> Several factors, including geography, sex, social class, race, and high school record, have much more to do with who goes where to college than do college entrance tests, of which the SAT is only one. . . . However, all these determinants are interconnected, and the College Board's program of tests, if not the most important of them, is certainly one of the most salient. The tests are therefore a sort of lightning rod, which results in their drawing both useful criticism and criticism that could with more effect be directed elsewhere, but which also results in their being a convenient focus for discussion of the entire college entrance process and its implications for education generally and for society at large. (51)

In the remaining pages of this chapter, the College Board tests provide this "convenient focus" for my discussion of the academy's institutionalization of literacy through twentieth-century developments in literacy testing at the college entrance level. College Board tests and policy statements therefore provide the bulk of material from which I draw conclusions about developments in such testing. As in previous chapters, however, the discussion is not directed so much toward uncovering the history of the College Board or of any other individual testing agency as toward the discovery of social conditions and attitudes that underlie the academically sanctioned definition of literacy and the ways in which the discipline of English studies has institutionalized a particular academic version of literacy through college entrance examinations in the field of their professional expertise.

Especially noteworthy among the social changes to which the College Board's tests and policies responded during the early twentieth century was a growing respect for science and technology and for the scientific method of acquiring knowledge. That respect was inspired in part by the obvious contributions of science and technology to America's wartime effort and by America's arrival, after the Second World War, at a position of global influence. That particular influence was experienced directly and concretely on American campuses during World War I, when the academy's contribution to the wartime cause was the donation of university campuses and facilities to the education of military personnel and the training of skilled civilian workers. Woodrow Wilson advertised higher education as a patriotic duty, realizing that the nation's success in the war and its economic aftermath would depend upon advanced technology and a work force trained to handle it.

The administrative and economic consequences of direct campus involvement in America's war effort were profound. The war years set the precedent of academic departments "hiring themselves out" to the federal government, a practice which in the immediately postwar era evolved into the founding of several agencies for centralizing academic authority, in part through coordinating federal and private educational funding agencies. Foremost among these were the National Research Council (NRC), and the American Council of Education (ACE). The latter is of particular significance because its direct involvement in the educational testing movement immediately after the war eventually resulted in that branch of the ACE becoming a part of the Educational Testing Service (ETS), founded in 1947 to take over the development, administration, scoring, and interpretation of

College Board exams. As we shall discover, the centralization of academic authority that replaced what has been described as a "non-system" of decentralized campus authorities has proven especially profitable for academic disciplines whose fields intersect national economic and political interests. Fields of scientific research, along with engineering and other applied sciences, that had experienced their first growth spurts at the turn of the century grew to vigorous young maturity with the United States' entry into World War I, nourished largely by external funding. Business, too, found its way into the academy in the postwar years as industrialization and the country's entry into the international trade market created demands for an increasingly complex business structure and more sophisticated economic theory.

Bowles and Pearson, reporting on behalf of the College Board, maintain that during the twenties and thirties the College Board began to recognize and eventually accept a much different role in the admissions process than the one for which it had originally been founded. Carefully articulated in Bowles and Pearson's account in the rhetoric of public service, the College Board's transformation during that time derived from an implicit change in leadership in accord with the centralization process described above. Initially guided by representatives of discreet academic institutions, primarily those in the East, the board, over the course of these two decades, came to place its trust in the ideal of public education, an ideal that was by then to a large extent focused upon national rather than local economic interests.

Before the elimination of comprehensive achievement examinations in 1942, they explain, the board's entrance examinations and supporting syllabi and reading lists reflected a conscious effort on the part of the College Board "to prescribe the nature of academic preparation in behalf of the colleges it represented" (23). By the 1920s and 1930s, however, the board gradually came to recognize that its prescriptive purpose, dictated in large part by endowed private colleges and preparatory schools in the East, was at odds with the national goal of developing a public school system that would meet the needs of a wide variety of students. From 1941 on, then, the board officially declared that its tests were not intended to "prescribe or influence classroom instruction" (23), but they were intended to serve the needs of the American academy as a unified entity.

In the field of English studies, which initially had identified itself at the center of modern liberal arts education, this meant that examiners were forced to acknowledge that the nonliterary student identified by the College Board's Committee on English was entitled to a place in higher education. As a result, the entrance examinations in English changed in ways that made them more amenable to the interests and aptitudes of these nontraditional college students whose academic inclinations connected them more firmly than imaginative literary students with national interests.

Closely related to the academy's blossoming admiration for applied science and the scientific method of investigation was the rapid growth of educational psychology and the ways in which its contributions revolutionized educational philosophy in this country. From the beginning, educational psychology was a discipline that relied heavily upon empirical studies and statistical measurement in order to bring scientific accuracy and precision to educational studies. As Applebee has pointed out, during the period between the wars, science was popularly identified with efficiency, in part because of the model of "scientific management" adopted by American business. Closely connected with the ideal of scientific management in the schools was a widespread enthusiasm for the scientific-measurement movement in education (Applebee, *Tradition* 80–81), a movement spearheaded in the United States by such individuals as E. L. Thorndike and J. M. Stalnaker. Applebee reproduces the following memorable quotation to illustrate the fervor of Thorndike's conviction that "rational change" in education depended upon accurate measurement of educational "products":

> Whatever exists at all exists in some amount. To know it thoroughly involves knowing its quantity as well as its quality. Education is concerned with changes in human beings; a change is a difference between two conditions; each of these conditions is known to us only by the products produced by it—things made, words spoken, acts performed, and the like. . . . To measure a product well means so to define its amount that competent persons will know

how large it is, with some precision, and that this knowledge may be recorded and used. This is the general *Credo* of those who, in the last decade, have been busy trying to extend and improve measurements of educational products. (78)

Aptitude, Objectivity, and English Studies

As colleges and testing agencies faced the challenge of efficiently processing increasing numbers of college applicants, it became apparent that traditional essay testing methods were no longer feasible in terms of time and money. The alternative—new-type examinations developed by psychometricians—met the academy's needs in a number of different ways. First, because objective examinations required no special expertise on the part of scorers, they could be processed rapidly and cheaply, initially through the use of relatively unskilled laborers and later on, with the progress of computer technology in the 1950s, by machine. Second, by eliminating the need for value judgments in scoring, objective examinations gave the appearance, at least, of being more fair and impartial than essay examinations, and thus complied with America's desire to perceive the academy as a democratic institution. Finally, because of their presumed ojectivity and because the results of the exams could easily be translated into statistical terms, objective examinations, themselves the products of "scientific" advances in the academy, satisfied demands for modern, efficient methods and precise, scientific measurements. Faith in the scientific accuracy and precision of exams such as the SAT was further reinforced by validity studies like Thorndike's, which showed the predictive power of aptitude exams and intelligence tests to exceed that of traditional essay exams (see Bowles 14; Fuess 197–98).

In the field of English studies, the various trends in testing noted above have proved especially problematic. Statistical studies had demonstrated that the verbal portion of the SAT, when used in conjunction with other measures such as the high school record, was a more accurate predictor of a student's success in college English courses than were the traditional essay examinations in English administered by the College Board or by individual colleges and universities. The College Board's Commission on English acknowledged this finding in its 1931 report but, voicing the fears of a good many English teachers and professors clinging fast to the ideal of liberal education, maintained that the essay examinations should nevertheless be retained because they promoted certain cultural values that an objective test overlooked. "The question is not so much a result reducible to statistics," the commission argued, "as it is a determination to retain in American education certain factors contributing to civilization and culture rather than to the mechanical efficiency of the American college student" (Commission on English 153–54).

In an effort to further justify retention of essay entrance examinations in English, the commission attempted to identify specific skills not tapped by the SAT and recommended that those skills become the focal point of the College Board's future essay examinations in English:

> The Scholastic Aptitude Test, as has been already said, analyzes thoroughly the candidate's power to read and interpret prose, to identify definitions, and to show his knowledge of the meaning of words. The test covers a portion of the definition of the requirements for the Comprehensive Examination in English which is designed to measure "the candidate's ability to think for himself and to apply what he has learned to the interpretations of passages of literature which he has not read before." It does not, however, test the candidate's ability to paraphrase or to make a précis, or to interpret the subtler qualities of a poem read at sight. This fact would raise the question, therefore, whether for the future Part II of the Comprehensive English paper should be confined to paraphrase and precise writing, together with sight interpretations of poetry. (Commission on English 154)

A review of the College Board's Comprehensive Examination in English during the 1930s indicates that the board examiners did indeed take the commission's suggestions to heart by supplying exams emphasizing literary study and sight interpretations of both prose and poetry, as well as paraphrase and summary tasks. An immediate effect of the College Board's support for new-type exams, then, was to diminish the academic terrain that came under direct control of English studies specialists so long as they maintained strict professional autonomy within the academy. The SAT's apparent success as an instrument that could define academic aptitude, a construct tightly interwoven with what Cook-Gumperz would later term the "essential product of education" signified a partial surrender of the right to define academic literacy to psychometricians whose professional loyalties were by no means guaranteed to coincide with those of English studies specialists.

Although the board's recognition of the nonliterary student had led to a gradual loosening of a strictly literary definition of English studies during the first two decades of the century, the thirties witnessed a certain reversal of that trend, as the profession, in a sense, circled its liberal education wagons in the face of a "scientific" invasion of its territory. To observe the latter trend we need only take a comparative look at the restricted and comprehensive forms of the English entrance examination. Until its demise in the mid-1930s, the composition section of the restricted form continued to feature nonliterary topic choices that required students to draw upon their own immediate experiences rather than their reading. The 1934 Restricted Examination, for instance, includes only two "reading" topics—"Dollar books" and "Keeping up with the authors"—among fourteen other options, of which the following are typical: "Telephone pests," "Let me show you," "The dividends of a good hobby," "My uses for the out of doors," "On not being ashamed to be thrifty," "When work becomes a privilege," "When leisure becomes a problem," and "The recipe says it's delicious."

Meanwhile, the Comprehensive Examination, which as we recall was by far the more popular and widely used form, focused more and more exclusively on literary topics throughout the thirties, eventually discontinuing the final composition section of the exam and incorporating extended theme writing—often in the form of paraphrase or summary—into the sections devoted to literary appreciation, literary analysis, and reading comprehension.

In 1931, for instance, the list of ten composition topics in the final section of the June Comprehensive Examination included as options four quotations: "Music, when soft voices die, / Vibrates in the memory—," "The past is the tradition of the present; the present therefore is the tradition of the future," "We left behind the painted buoy / That tosses at the harbour-mouth," and "Experience is the best school; but a good school is a great experience." Two of the quotations, being in the form of poetry, can be classified as literary prompts; the other two, more akin to maxims, recall the device of the Commonplace Book, used for invention purposes by writers from the Renaissance onward. While not explicitly literary in the same sense as the poetry prompts, then, they nevertheless exemplify the literary inclination to contemplate symbolic rather than material reality. In that sense, the use of a textual prompt rather than a reference to the writer's own lived experience to generate the intellectual substance of additional text emphasizes the priority of book life over real life.

Two other options in the 1931 list of composition topics require students to speculate on the meaning and purpose of literature: "Aristotle said that great poetry is more true than history" and "Literature: record, interpretation, or escape?" Two more topic possibilities, "A rocky pool" and "Silence," might also qualify as poetic, particularly when placed, as they are in the 1931 Comprehensive Examination, immediately after two sections that focus on the poetry of Wordsworth and Coleridge. (Interestingly enough, the Comprehensive Examination for June 1936 asks questions about a poem entitled "Silence" by Thomas Hood, which is reproduced in the text of the exam.) Of the ten composition topics on the 1931 exam, then, it may be argued that only two can be called purely nonliterary.

Succeeding years produced exams featuring a preponderance of literary composition topics. In 1932, seven out of twelve topics were either quotations or prompts relating to literary genre, authors, or literary education. Among the remaining five topics that year, at least one, "A night sky," is likely to call forth poetic discourse. The list of composition topics for June 1933 was similar in nature, with a proportionately large number of literary topics. In both June and September of 1934, however, all composition topics on the Comprehensive Examinations were either quotations or statements about literature. The following two years saw a mix of literary and nonliterary topics in the composition section, but in 1937 the College Board adopted a new format for the Comprehensive Examination in English that reduced the list of composition topics to only one option, and that a literary topic. That revision effectively began to eliminate the distinction that had once clearly existed between the literature and composition sections of the examination. Except for specifying a considerably greater length than was required by the other five questions of the examination, the composition prompt reads very much like a typical "literature question," with its reference to a quoted passage and its request that students relate the ideas in that passage to their reading. After reproducing a passage from Henry van Dyke's *The Ruling Passion,* the 1937 examination asks students to write their own essays entitled "The Ruling Passion," developing and illustrating the ideas presented in van Dyke's passage by focusing on characters from their reading in history, biography, or literature. A similar type of composition topic appears in the 1938 Comprehensive Examination, but in 1939 and succeeding years, no separate composition section is featured, although all of the questions on the exams require the student to do a considerable amount of writing.

In addition to becoming more exclusively literary throughout the thirties, the Comprehensive Examination came to include an increasing amount of quoted material that students presumably had not encountered before. The exam also featured a growing number of questions requiring students to produce paraphrases and summaries of the passages that had been reproduced. The June 1938 Comprehensive Examination is particularly revealing in its opening prompt: "It has been said that perhaps the best test of intelligent reading is the capacity for making a good summary." This statement is immediately followed by a request that students produce summaries (75–100 words) of two novels and two plays of their own choosing. The test then provides a model summary of *Silas Marner.* In the course of the decade, the passages for summary and paraphrase steadily increased in length, growing from short poems and single-paragraph prose pieces to prose and poetry passages of two or more pages in length.

Clearly the examiners intended the Comprehensive Examination to be a test of power rather than mastery of the form and content of certain literary works. Instructions to students taking the exams between 1932 and 1941 open with a clarification of purpose that reads: "Every question on this examination tests your power in reading and composition" (1932–33) or "Every question is a test of power in reading and writing" (1934–41). In keeping with the commission's definition of *power* as the ability to apply reading and writing skills to new situations—that is, to the reading, comprehension, and interpretation of texts never before encountered—the Comprehensive Examinations of the thirties reproduced a great many passages, both prose and poetry, in the pages of the exam. No longer did the exams require students to discourse on texts they retained in memory, but they engaged students in the reading of previously unencountered texts, thereby requiring them to apply their literacy skills to the purpose of demonstrating comprehension and appreciation of literary writing.

By far the majority of the quoted passages in these prompts were from the works of recognized literary authors or of literary critics. Questions relating to the passages, then, typically asked students to perform one of two types of literacy tasks—on the one hand, to interpret or analyze the texts of literary authors and, on the other, to apply literary critics' statements about various aspects of literary discourse to their own reading experience.

An example that typifies the former question type appears in the second question on the June 1935 Comprehensive Examination. The question opens with a reproduction of an excerpt from Dorothy Wordsworth's diary in which she tells of her brother writing a poem that describes the sounds and sights the two of them had encountered on a recent walk in the countryside. She then produces her own description of the same sounds and sights. Immediately thereafter, William Wordsworth's finished poem is reproduced, and students are asked to "compare the arrangement of the descriptive details in the prose with their arrangement in the poem." Having done this, students are to answer the following questions: "In what ways, such as order of details and manner of expression, do the two selections differ? Which selection do you prefer? Give reasons."

The second type of frequently occurring writing prompt is typified by the second question on the June 1932 Comprehensive Examination. This prompt opens with a quoted passage from Gilbert Murray's *Literature as Revelation:* "The value of literature is not in conveying a new piece of information; its value lies in its power of suddenly directing your attention, and the whole focus of your attention and imagination, towards a particular part of life." Following this quotation is the request, "Discuss, in the light of this passage, three works that you have read (fiction, non-fiction, poetry, or drama)."

By focusing the Comprehensive Examination on aspects of English studies that the SAT and objective achievement tests were either unable to measure or simply were not designed to assess, the board evidently hoped to legitimize the continued use of essay examinations, at least in the field of English. Ultimately, however, its efforts to that end were unsuccessful, largely because essay examinations were proving too costly and too time-consuming to use with the steadily increasing numbers of college applicants the board was having to process. When in 1942 the Comprehensive Examination was finally eliminated altogether, the protests of English teachers echoed the fears earlier voiced by the College Board's Commission on English. As Frank Bowles noted, many complained that the standards of college preparation suffered irreparable damage after 1942 (66). Fuess reports that teachers were especially concerned that literary instruction would suffer, since reliance on the SAT meant, at least according to the example set by College Board exams, that English studies had virtually been reduced to a subject without content (158).

College Board records of the period chronicle a long and bitter dispute between English teachers who were loathe to relinquish values they viewed as central to the liberal arts tradition and even to Western culture itself and psychometricians who represented a powerful scientific community within the academy. As Donlan reports, English teachers so adamantly protested the discontinuation of the Comprehensive Examination that the College Board was forced to reinstate an essay-type English composition exam in its battery of achievement tests during the years 1945–47. The exam, which consisted of a single essay on an assigned topic, written during a one-hour period, was a short-lived addition, however, and it was generally regarded by College Board examiners as the most controversial item in the achievement test battery. Fuess describes the Comprehensive Examination in English as "the *bete noir* of the Research Department" where it was contemptuously considered an "anachronism" because it failed to meet reliability standards set by the board. "The scientific experts," according to Fuess, regarded the exam as "a demonstration of the inadequacy and inaccuracy of human judgments as contrasted with the efficiency of mechanical checking" (180–81), and researchers publicly declared that "the problems involved in developing a reliable essay examination are, if not unsolveable, at least far from solved at the present time" (180).

J. M. Stalnaker, then Assistant Secretary of the College Board and a nationally renowned psychometrician both during and after the war, was an especially influential spokesman for the exclusive use of objective tests on the basis of their contributions to the scientific improvement of education. In support of the board's decision to discontinue essay testing in 1942, he wrote:

> The type of test so highly valued by teachers of English, which requires the candidate to write a theme or essay, is not a worth-while testing device. Whether or not the writing of essays as a means of teaching writing deserves the place it has in the secondary school curriculum may be equally questioned. Eventually, it is hoped, sufficient evidence may be accumulated to outlaw forever the "write-a-theme-on" . . . type of examination. (qtd. in Fuess 158)

Stalnaker's stated desire to abolish essay testing found support from College Board administrators who were growing increasingly concerned not only at the poor scoring reliability of such exams but also at their excessive cost. In 1946, after the reinstatement of a one-hour composition test, the board reported that the cost of scoring the English Composition Test was $50,000 per year—twice the amount of the board's total research expenditures for the same year (Fuess 197). To test the validity of such expense for a single exam, the board conducted experiments with a test covering three possible measures of college-entry literacy skills: an objective test focused primarily on points of grammar, mechanics, and usage; a traditional essay test; and a test requiring students to revise awkward and faultily constructed paragraphs. Of the three, the objective test correlated highest with predictability measures such as college grades in freshman English classes (Fuess 198). These results, coupled with the high cost of administering the exam and the poor reliability of essay scoring, seemed to justify the board's decision to discontinue the English Composition Test in 1948, after only three years of use.

But the decision was not satisfactory to all parties involved. English teachers continued to protest that essay writing and essay testing made valuable contributions to American education—that they instilled values and emphasized skills that would be lost if preparation for college were to be geared solely toward the taking of objective tests. Fuess observes that in the late forties, the weight of opinion remained with essay tests, even though the weight of evidence was on the side of objective examinations (198).

In part, the protest of English teachers against objective examinations was a protest against a newly developing definition of literacy that these exams seemed to be promoting. In earlier years they had endorsed an inclination to perceive college-entry literacy as power rather than as the mere mastery of a narrowly defined body of knowledge about language and literature. Their revised notion of literacy as power, however, was still a definition that tied college-entry literacy to the cultural values contained in "good" literature and the "correct" use of written language. Implicit in this definition was the assumption that truly literate applicants to college could appreciate good literature, could distinguish between good and inferior works of literature, and could identify connections between the ideas and values presented in good literature and those that governed their own lives. As changing social conditions mandated the examiners' recognition of a less literary brand of literacy, however, the meaning of *power* accordingly broadened until it referred more to "general intelligence" than to dimensions of literary appreciation.

The proposal that literacy somehow equates with human intelligence was, of course, not entirely new to the academic community. In fact, underlying the logic of the traditional essay exam itself is the long-standing belief that written language is a fairly accurate representation of thought. Horace Mann's claim in 1845 that written examinations served as a "Daguerreotype likeness" of the "state and condition of pupils' minds" (334) and the belief of early psychometrician F. Y. Edgeworth that in evaluating students' written texts examiners were in fact measuring "intellectual worth" are but two of many testimonials to the established acceptability of this equation. Because the assumption was already a well-accepted bias in the academic community, English teachers were not so much disturbed by the notion that literacy skills were a measure of general intelligence as they were by the scientific derivation and the utilitarian motivations behind the new mechanistic definition of *intelligence* offered by the statisticians.

As a scientific construct, intelligence consisted of various discrete skills and abilities that could be measured separately from one another. These individual measurements could then be summed together to produce a presumably undistorted measure of general intelligence, or mental ability, or aptitude. In accordance with this construct, intelligence tests typically consisted of several sections, each of which was designed to measure an individual's ability to perform a particular type of mental operation—e.g., encoding or decoding meaning, perceiving similarity, perceiving difference, perceiving spatial relationships, and so forth.

Scholastic Aptitude and the Separate Measure of Reading and Writing

Within the College Board's test battery, the SAT has represented the new analytic approach to the measurement of intellectual operations from 1926 to the present. The earliest SAT exams (1926 and 1927), for instance, derived a composite "scholastic aptitude" score from nine subscores obtained from the student's performance on nine separate tasks: definitions, classifications, word arithmetic problems, artificial language, antonyms, number series completion, analogies, logical inference (deriving conclusions from premises and vice versa), and paragraph reading (in which students had to identify an inappropriate word that contradicted or otherwise disrupted the meaning of the paragraph) (Loret 96).

The same type of analytic approach to reading and writing skills, however, also characterized the objective composition tests that, initially at least, posed more direct competition to the traditional essay exam in English. The earliest of these required students to make correct choices in grammar, mechanics, and usage items; to edit errors from "incorrect" sentences or paragraphs; to arrange material effectively in paragraphs; and to identify topic sentences or select one from several sentences offered as summaries or paraphrases of a passage reproduced in the test. Some examiners argued that this analytic approach to measurement was generally a progressive step because it produced a fuller, more detailed and accurate "picture" of the examinee's academic achievements and scholastic aptitudes. In what seems to be an updated version of Mann's "Daguerreotype image" metaphor, College Board director Frank Bowles claimed in 1948 that "the objective tests with their large number of items and wide sampling of subject matter provide an 'album of candid shots' as compared with the 'eight or ten posed photographs' of the former essay examinations" (qtd. in Fuess 196).

But even a staunch supporter of objective tests like Bowles could not overlook the continuing protests of the English studies profession. Acknowledging that English composition perhaps constituted a special case, being a subject that could not be satisfactorily approached analytically, he spoke of "the nagging conviction that in English composition, the whole is more than the sum of its parts." Expanding upon this possibility and its implications for testing policies, he continued:

> If there were a reasonable chance of isolating, as factors subject to objective testing and objective judgment, *all* of the parts, and if there were an agreement that the whole was equal to the sum of its parts, then there would be conclusive argument for objective testing. However, until such isolation has been completed, and such agreement has been reached, the Board is obliged to consider the possibility of testing ability to write English by having the candidate write English. (qtd. in Fuess 198)

The history of college entrance testing in English since World War II, then, has consisted largely of various efforts on the part of examiners and educators to resolve conflicting academic notions about literacy. On the one hand, the definition implicit in objective, analytic measures of reading and writing projects literacy as a composite of skills and abilities that may be separated for scrutiny and reassembled. On the other hand, essay examinations that must be graded holistically assume that literacy is, as Bowles speculated, more than the sum of its parts.

Since World War II, the evolution of entrance examinations in English led by the nation's two most prominent college entrance testing agencies, the College Board and American College Testing (ACT), reflect a transfer of the power to control the definition of literacy as an academic product from the English departments of individual colleges and universities to centralized agencies supported by federal and corporate funding. The restructuring process has served to further reinforce the separation of reading and composition. As we have observed in the record of early College Board exams, that development was already underway in the early part of the century, but its progress was hastened immeasurably by the compartmentalizing forces of bureaucratic takeover. By testing reading primarily under the rubric of "verbal aptitude" while classifying writing skill as "achievement," the College Board, during the latter half of the twentieth century, has essentially separated those abilities into two nonoverlapping fields of ability. Achievement tests in literature disappeared from the picture entirely after 1941 and were not reinstated until 1968 (Donlan 90). By that time, achievement tests had acquired the status of optional exams, used mainly for placement rather than for admissions decisions.

While some colleges have in the past or continue today to require students to submit scores for specified achievement tests, the vast majority either do not require them at all or require only that students submit scores from a specified number of elective achievement tests. Donlan notes that during the 1956–57 academic year three college applicants took the SAT for every one who took one or more achievement tests. By 1977, the disproportion had grown to five SAT takers to every one applicant taking achievement tests (4). Statistics gathered in a study conducted by the American Association of Collegiate Registrars and Admissions Officers in conjunction with the College Board (1980) confirm the declining importance of achievement tests in American college admissions decisions. Of all the institutions surveyed in that study, 70 percent required admissions test scores in the form of the SAT or the ACT; 90 percent of the four-year public institutions and 84 percent of the four-year private institutions made this requirement. Meanwhile, only 11 percent of all the institutions surveyed required achievement test scores; 12 percent of the public four-year schools and 15 percent of the private four-year schools surveyed imposed that requirement. Viewed in another light, the relative importance of aptitude and achievement test scores is revealed in the same study by statistics indicating that 71 percent of all the institutions surveyed considered aptitude test scores (SAT, ACT, PSAT/NMSQT—Preliminary SAT/National Merit Scholarship Qualifying Test) to be either the most important factor (2 percent), a very important factor (42 percent), or one of several important factors (27 percent) in admissions decisions, whereas only 25 percent reported the same regard for achievement test scores: most important factor,

1 percent; very important, 5 percent; one of several important factors, 19 percent (17).

As the achievement tests, including the test of literature, thus fell from power, vocabulary and reading comprehension sections of the SAT verbal tests have increasingly carried the burden of assessing the reading skills of college applicants. At various times during the past forty-five years, the College Board has offered English Composition Tests that have employed direct (i.e., essay) measures of writing skills, but for a variety of reasons (e.g., poor rater reliability, excessive cost in terms of time and money), direct measurement of writing skills has not been consistently used in the College Board's English Composition Tests. At times, the exam has assumed a strictly objective format, and at other times it has experimented with alternative forms—such as interlinear writing—in an attempt to arrive at some compromise between indirect and direct assessment, but such experiments have generally been short-lived.

CHAPTER SIX

Reading and Writing in the Age of Objective Testing

The SAT, first used in 1926, was originally intended to provide supplementary information to help college admissions officials interpret the high school records and achievement test scores of applicants. Because it was purportedly "curriculum free," the SAT was expected to provide an assessment of applicants' academic promise and potential to succeed in college even when their limited exposure to specific subject areas might lead to poor performance on achievement tests. As we have seen, however, more recent years have witnessed the SAT's virtual replacement of achievement test scores, and as College Board spokesman Thomas Donlan observed in 1984, "the supplemental nature of the SAT . . . is often forgotten" (37).

Because creation of the Scholastic Aptitude Test was stimulated by developments in the testing of "general intelligence," the earliest forms of the exam yielded scores that made no distinction between verbal and mathematical abilities. In 1928, however, Carl C. Brigham, creator of the SAT, argued that verbal and mathematical aptitudes were sufficiently different from one another that more precise and accurate information could be conveyed to admissions boards if scholastic aptitude scores were analyzed into separate verbal and mathematical components. This has continued to be the procedure for obtaining and reporting scholastic aptitude scores to the present day, with the exception of a six-year period, 1936–41, when only verbal items were featured on the SAT, and a separate mathematical attainment test was administered for a separate score.

Form of the Verbal SAT

Of the nine subtests comprising the first SAT, seven contained verbal item types. "Antonyms" required students to choose from six options the term most nearly opposite in meaning to a given term; "Analogies" required the selection of a fourth term to complete the formula, Term A : Term B = Term C : ?; "Paragraph reading" involved crossing out an inappropriate word or phrase that conflicted with the meaning or tone of the paragraph; "Definitions" required students to select from a list words that correctly completed sentence definitions of certain terms; "Classifications" involved selection from a list of six terms the three most closely related to one another in meaning; "Artificial language" provided grammar rules and vocabulary items for a made-up language and asked students to translate phrases from English into the artificial language and vice versa; and "Logical inference" provided data or premises and asked students to identify the truth status of conclusions based on those data or premises.

Donlan explains that the years 1926 to 1930 marked a period of experimentation, during which the composition of the SAT verbal section varied considerably. At the end of the period, the test stabilized somewhat with three item types: antonyms, paragraph reading, and double definitions. When analogy was reintroduced in 1936, a basic format was established that has undergone only minor revisions up to the present day. The following are examples of each of the item types, drawn from various forms of the SAT used during the period 1928–43:

Antonyms: Directions to students read, "Remember that the symbol ^ means oppositeness. No synonyms are wanted, although they may be given as one of the wrong alternatives. The answer is always *opposite in meaning* to the given word."

   1. Find ADJECTIVE ^ adverb "unequivocally"
     (1. equal 2. whispered 3. composite 4. trustworthy
     5. ambiguous)

The above item was used in 1928, 1929, 1936, 1937, 1938, and 1939. (Loret 96).

Paragraph reading: Directions to students read, "In each of the following paragraphs, *one important* word, and one word only, has been substituted for another word and spoils the meaning of the paragraph. Find this word and blacken it."

   1. In theory, every person charged with authority should
     give his subordinates the minimum possible freedom,
     for it is conceded that men do not work their best

when confined in strait-jackets. Some executives carry this theory into practice, usually with notable success.

50. Thomas Carlyle fought a giant Despair all his life, and never gave an inch of ground. Indeed, so far as the upshot of his death was concerned, the amount of work actually done and its value as a tonic and a spur of noble endeavor of all kinds were tremendous.

The above items were used on Form I of the 1934 SAT (Loret 11).

Double definitions: Instructions to students read, "From each definition on this page, *two words* have been omitted. The first word is among the first four key words, numbered 1, 2, 3, or 4, and the last word omitted is among the last four words, numbered 5, 6, 7, or 8. Write the numbers of the *two words which best complete each definition* in the space in the margin."

1. _____ is the act or process of gaining _____ of something.
   1. acquisition 2. acquiescence 3. gravitation 4. velocity 5. possession 6. weight 7. momentum 8. permission

25. A _____ is a venerable leader ruling by _____ right.
    1. mayor 2. patriarch 3. minister 4. general 5. paternal 6. military 7. ceremonial 8. electoral

50. A _____ is a voiced or whispered sound uttered with but slight obstruction in the _____ passage.
    1. trochee 2. twang 3. chant 4. vowel
    5. accented 6. oral 7. musical 8. nasal

The above items appeared on Form I of the 1934 SAT (Loret 10).

Analogy: Instructions to students read, "Each of the following questions consists of two words which have a certain relation to one another, followed by five numbered pairs of related words. Decide in which numbered pair the two words have a relationship most nearly like that between the first two words. Then underline the number on the answer sheet which corresponds to the pair you've selected."

1. OFFSPRING : PARENT:
   1. book : reader 2. book : author 3. book : teacher
   4. pride : author 5. pride : workman

25. SECOND : ETERNITY:
    1. point : ambiguous 2. point : continuum 3. ambiguous : unequivocal 4. now : continuum 5. now : then
50. DAY : NIGHT:
    1. intrepidity : pusillanimity 2. intrepidity : benevolence 3. intrepidity : restitution 4. simony : benevolence 5. benevolence : restitution

The above items originally appeared on Form R of the 1943 SAT (Loret 12).

Between 1941 and 1946 the double-definition item type was altered to become the modern sentence-completion type, and between 1945 and 1946, the paragraph-reading item type was transformed into the currently used reading-comprehension type of question. Examples of the revised types are as follows:

Sentence completion: Instructions to students read, "In each of the sentences in this subtest there is a blank space, indicating that a word has been omitted. Beneath the sentence are five numbered words; from these five words you are to choose the one word which, when inserted in the blank space *best* fits in with the meaning of the sentence as a whole."

14. One of the most prevalent erroneous contentions is that Argentina is a country of _____ agricultural resources and needs only the arrival of ambitious settlers.
    1. modernized 2. flourishing 3. undeveloped
    4. waning 5. limited

15. The last official statistics for the two indicated the presence of 24,212 Italians, 6,450 Magyars, and 2,315 Germans, which insures to the _____ a relative preponderance.
    1. Germans 2. figures 3. town 4. Magyars
    5. Italians

16. Precision of wording is necessary in good writing; by choosing words that exactly convey the desired meaning, one can avoid _____.
    1. duplicity 2. incongruity 3. complexity 4. ambiguity 5. implications

17. Various civilians of the liberal school in the British Parliament remonstrated that there were no grounds

for _____ of French aggression, since the Emperor
showed less disposition to augment the navy than had
Louis Philippe.
1. suppression 2. retaliation 3. apprehension
4. concealment 5. commencement

The four above items appeared as sample questions in the *Bulletin of
Information* published by the College Entrance Examination Board
to help students prepare for the 1947–48 SAT's (10).

Reading comprehension: Instructions to students read, "In this
subtest each passage is followed by questions based upon its content.
After reading a passage, answer each of the questions following it by
choosing the correct completion and blackening the space beneath
the corresponding number on the answer sheet.

"The questions following a passage are to be answered on the basis
of what is *stated* or *implied* in that passage."

Verbal material is the vehicle by which the mind thinks.
Visual images of the phenomena, it is true, may sometimes
be of help in clarifying abstract concepts in such fields as
physics and geometry, but these images are never completely
self-sufficient.

The truth is that after the beginning of adolescence words
must constitute a large part, and an increasingly large part as
life advances, of what the human being has to learn. This
brings up the issue of verbal memorizing. The more accurately words are learned, the better, if only the teacher makes
sure that what they *signify* is also understood. It is the failure
of this latter condition in so much old-fashioned recitation
that has caused that reaction against parrot-like reproduction
which we are so familiar with today. A friend of mine, vis-
iting a school, was asked to examine a young class in geography. Glancing at the book, she said, "Suppose you should
dig a hole in the ground, hundreds of feet deep, how would
you find it at the bottom, warmer or colder than on top?"
None of the class replying, the teacher said, "I'm sure they
know, but I think you don't ask the question quite rightly."
So, taking the book, she asked, "In what condition is the interior of the globe?" and received the immediate answer:
"The interior of the globe is in a condition of igneous fusion." Better exclusive object teaching than such verbal reci-

tations as that; and yet verbal reproduction, intelligently handled, can surely play a leading part in education.

1. The author believes that the thinking process cannot
   1. function without the use of words
   2. function without visual images
   3. be injured by poor teaching methods
   4. change noticeably after adolescence
   5. be swayed by outside influences

2. The geography class in the illustration
   1. did not know anything about geography
   2. did not like the wording of the first question
   3. did not really understand what "igneous fusion" meant
   4. understood the basic principle involved in the question
   5. did not answer the first question because it was not related to what they had been studying

3. By "this latter condition" (line 9) the author means
   1. satisfactory recitation procedures
   2. training in verbal memorizing
   3. training in understanding words
   4. adequate training in scientific vocabulary
   5. increased use of words

4. Which of the following would the author of this passage *least* recommend that children learn in school?
   1. If a person is held under water for ten minutes without air, he will drown.
   2. The upper half of a room is generally warmer than the lower half because heat rises.
   3. If water is kept at the boiling temperature, it becomes steam.
   4. Aluminum is suitable for use in airplanes because it is one of the lightest metals.
   5. Pure iron is a silver white metallic element which is malleable and ductile.

The reading passage and questions above appeared as an example of what students could expect in the reading-comprehension section of the SAT. They were published in the College Entrance Examination Board's *Bulletin of Information*, 1952–53 (25–26).

Particularly short-lived among the item types first introduced were classification items (discontinued in 1928) and logical-inference and artificial-language items (both discontinued in 1927). Items similar to those that were early on eliminated from the College Board's Scholastic Aptitude Test, however, may well have remained in use in tests administered by individual colleges and universities. As late as 1953, *Time* magazine reviewed a study guide for students applying to Annapolis and West Point. According to the guide, West Point had for some time included in its entrance examination a series of questions based on an artificial language for which students were supplied a set of grammar rules and vocabulary items. The language changed from year to year, and the questions relating to it were purportedly designed to test the candidate's intelligence (Huppe and Kaminsky 95–96).

The SAT Verbal Test: Implications for Reading

To the extent that "verbal scholastic aptitude" as measured by a test composed of the item types contained in the SAT during its sixty-five years of existence encapsulates a definition of academic literacy skills, that definition involves at least two essential components. The first is an extensive vocabulary, acquired, as the College Board bulletins and commercial study guides explain to students, through extensive reading. The second is a working knowledge of the principles of formal logic, deriving from Aristotelian origins.

As one of the earliest (1947–48) College Entrance Examination Board bulletins makes clear, the background of reading and a working knowledge of formal logic were types of preparation for the SAT explicitly recommended by the board:

> The verbal section is designed to measure the candidate's understanding of words, his skill in dealing with word and thought relationships, and his ability to read with understanding and discrimination. A wide background in reading which has broadened the student's vocabulary will be an asset in this examination, but no outside information in the field of literature or any other specialized field of knowl-

edge is required. The candidate's score on this test depends largely on his functional vocabulary, his ability to reason logically, and his ability to combine ideas and to draw correct inferences. (7)

The importance of vocabulary is immediately obvious in such item types as definitions, analogies, antonyms, and paragraph reading or sentence completion, whereas classification, artificial language, and logical inference place apparent emphasis on logical reasoning. But even the items included in the first set, while they do indeed address vocabulary, do so by invoking a system of logical operations based on the perception of certain logical relationships such as opposition (antonyms), identity (definitions), contradiction or exclusivity (paragraph reading), and similarity (analogies).

The bias of formal logic and extensive reading in the definition of literacy that evidently has and continues to inform the construction of the verbal portion of the SAT coincides in many ways with Olson's description of "essayist" literacy in his study of the cognitive consequences of literacy. Like Olson himself, the tests reveal particular concern for "those consequences of literacy associated with mastery of the 'schooled' language of written texts" (258).

As we have seen, Olson falls squarely within the formalist camp of literacy theory. His observations focus exclusively on literacy in academic terms, and from those observations he develops a description of literacy as the ability to manipulate symbolic forms. According to Olson's descriptive study, meaning resides in the text, rather than in the dynamic comprised of writer and reading audience, and as a consequence, the ideal of academic literacy is a currency of "explicit, autonomous statements" that, when arranged in textual form, are logically consistent and self-referential.

Significant to the professional history of English studies, the definition of literacy that Olson articulates and that also emerges from the pages of the SAT emphasizes expository rather than literary texts. Such an emphasis is no doubt the inevitable result of English studies' tendency to view literature as an object of study rather than a model for academic discourse. Although students have been expected to read literature and to write about it, they have not been supposed capable of writing literary texts themselves, and indeed professors as well are typically critics rather than creators of literary texts. The conditions in English studies classrooms accordingly fostered the rise of the "literary theme," a subgenre of the expository essay in whose development Olson traces the history of academic literacy (see also Tuman, *Preface* 59–60).

As has already become apparent in the brief survey of SAT test item types that opens this chapter, Olson's formal definition of academic literacy in many ways coincides nicely with the verbal skills the SAT purports to assess. In particular, the test by its very format places high value on the reader's ability to decontextualize written texts— to divorce the text from the circumstances in which it was produced or read, focusing instead on the task of precisely determining the assertion made by each sentence of the text as well as the presuppositions and logical implications of those assertions. The ideal text, by the same token, depends upon the refinement of semantic explicitness through elimination of all possible sources of ambiguity—through adherence to the conventions of a standard written language. As Olson explains, "The attempt was to construct sentences for which the meaning was dictated by the lexical or syntactic features of the sentence itself. To this end, the meaning of terms had to be conventionalized by means of definitions, and the rules of implication had to be articulated and systematically applied" (270).

The bias of formal logic and rational modes of thought has long been apparent in item types that require students to perform linguistic operations dependent upon the recognition of logical relationships among terms. The ideal of autonomous text is further reinforced by the test's presentation of texts in isolation from a communicative context and apart from the student's prior knowledge of the subject matter treated in the text. Consider, for example, the following instructions, which introduced a "data interpretation" test item used on various forms of the verbal SAT between 1951 and 1956:

> This is a subtest to test your ability to draw conclusions or to make interpretations from data presented to you. In every case you are to assume that the data as given are true.
>
> Following each set of data you will find a number of statements. Study each statement carefully and *on the basis of the data alone*, decide on the degree of truth or falsity of the statement. In arriving at your decision, you are to con-

fine yourself to the data given, even though you may be acquainted with other evidence which indicates clearly whether the statement is true or false. (Loret 101)

Typical SAT instructions to students concerning reading-comprehension items likewise emphasize the ideal of the text's autonomy by disavowing any attempt on the part of test makers to engage students in an exchange of personally held ideas. Reading-comprehension items of SAT exams administered in 1986, for instance, are prefaced with an explanation that questions following the reading passage are based only on the content of that particular passage, followed by the direction, "Answer all questions following a passage on the basis of what is *stated* or *implied* in that passage" (College Board, *10 SAT's* 128).

Reading passages are also accompanied by a disclaimer of functional communicative intent:

> The reading passages in this test are brief excerpts or adaptations of excerpts from published materials. The ideas contained in them do not necessarily represent the opinions of the College Board or Educational Testing Service. To make the test suitable for testing purposes, we may in some cases have altered the style, contents, or point of view of the original. (128)

Similar disclaimers have been a long-standing feature of the reading-comprehension sections of the SAT. At least as early as 1960, Loret reports, both the College Board and its administrative agency, the Educational Testing Service, have explicitly disavowed responsibility for the propositional content of reading-comprehension items. As directions to students make clear, the reading passages are therefore to be regarded as texts that provide "significant problems for analysis and evaluation" (16) rather than a communication of authorial intent. The student, in other words, is to respond to the *form* rather than the *content* or purpose of the passage. The full disclaimer for the reading-comprehension item of the 1960 exam featured in Loret's historical survey of the SAT reads as follows:

> The passages for this test have been adapted from published material to provide the candidate with significant problems

for analysis and evaluation. The ideas contained in the passages are those of the original author and do not necessarily represent the opinions of the College Entrance Examination Board or Educational Testing Service. (16)

Because tests like the SAT assume a view of text as a primarily formal construct, autonomous in its isolation from a social context in which it might serve as a medium for the exchange of propositional content, students are typically given very little, or very often no information at all, about the rhetorical context in which the reading passages were originally produced or published. Almost without exception, passages are presented as autonomous creations, directed at no particular audience and intent on no particular purposeful exchange with the reader. Such information about original context as students are able to obtain, they must discern from clues supplied by the texts themselves.

Reading, according to the academic view of literacy, requires a familiarity with conventions of written text that reduce the normal ambiguity of oral language or even of highly "personal" or context-dependent written language. Olson voices the formalist bias when he explains that because written language must encode the nonlinguistic information of oral exchanges into an "enlarged set of explicit linguistic conventions," the written language required of essayist, or academic, literacy is "richer" than oral language. From that premise arise the evaluative criteria deemed appropriate to the assessment of academic literacy. According to the rules of the essay genre, Olson writes, "If unconventionalized or nonlinguistic knowledge is permitted to intrude, we charge the writer with reasoning via unspecified inferences and assumptions or the reader with misreading the text" ("Utterance" 272).

Elsewhere, Olson defines such reading as a "formal" or "counter-intuitive" process requiring readers to suspend their awareness of contradictory information or conflicting beliefs in order to extract meaning from the text. This reading contrasts sharply, he explains, with the process we employ in the comprehension of oral or poetic texts in which "statements match, in an often tantalizing way, the expectancies and experiences of the listener" (277). In the academic genre of expository discourse, however, the processing of prose text follows rules that are radically different. As Olson explains, reading and writing in this genre "appeals to premises and rules of logic for deriving implications":

> Whether or not the premise corresponds to common sense is irrelevant. All that is critical is that the premises are explicit and the inferences correctly drawn. The appeal is formal rather than intuitive. As a consequence, the criterion for the success of a statement in explicit prose text is its formal structure; if the text is formally adequate and the reader fails to understand, that is the reader's problem. The meaning is in the text. (277)

Composition Tests in an Age of Objective Examinations

The SAT verbal exam virtually took over the College Board's testing of reading ability for college applicants after World War II, and since then has served consistently in that capacity, but the board's efforts to measure writing ability have been considerably more complicated and controversial. Donlan, summarizing the board's attempts to devise a means of assessing writing skills that is both valid and reliable, mentions the traditional essay exam (with and without a literary bias); the all-multiple-choice English Composition Achievement Test; the "free-response interlinear exercise" and a twenty-minute essay response section added to an otherwise objective composition test; the two-hour all-essay General Composition Test; the Writing Sample (administered by the College Board, but scored by individual colleges to which the student had applied; and most recently, the Test of Standard Written English (TSWE) used to supplement the SAT and achievement tests, primarily as a placement instrument (69).

The primary impetus behind the discontinuation of essay exams was pragmatic rather than ideological; the administration and scoring of essay exams were too time-consuming and costly to fit the accelerated wartime academic schedule adopted by the board in the 1940s. The subsequent decision to rely upon objective achievement tests and the SAT as college entrance exams, however, found overwhelming support among statisticians who, because of the board's wartime activities in the service of the federal government and the armed forces, had become a strong and influential force in determining

College Board procedures. Against the judgment of those statisticians, the board agreed to reinstate a greatly modified version of the essay composition test immediately after the war. The only essay test given by the College Board, the postwar composition test, was now completely free of literary content and, as a one-hour test, involved students in far less actual writing than the original three-hour achievement tests had required.

Scoring procedures for the exam, too, were greatly revised. Whereas the evaluation of English studies essay examinations as described by the Commission on English in 1931 was essentially a holistic activity, requiring examiners to assign scores on the basis of their general impressions of a student's written performance, examiners who scored the revised English composition test between 1945 and 1947 were instructed to evaluate student texts analytically, on the basis of seven to nine specified components of writing ability— for example, diction, spelling, and organization of material (Godshalk et al. iv).

No doubt the analytic approach to writing assessment was the product of many of the same influences that led to the SAT's analytic assessment of reading ability. Legitimated by the scientific-management philosophy of education, the analytic approach theoretically yielded a more accurate and precise measurement because it operated on a more precisely articulated definition of the phenomenon being measured. But despite the effort to bring scientific precision to the direct assessment of writing ability, the one-hour essay composition test was finally discontinued after 1947 on the grounds that it could not be scored reliably enough to meet the standards that the board had come to demand on the basis of reliability studies conducted on its objective tests.

Although its inclusion in the College Board's battery of admissions tests was short-lived, the one-hour essay English Composition Test embodies an implicit definition of academic literacy that remained fairly stable throughout many revisions in the board's testing of writing ability. Predictably, the composition test was consistent with the verbal SAT in privileging the production of autonomous expository texts in which the principles of formal logic play an important structuring role.

In its *Bulletin of Information,* the College Board made a nod in the direction of English studies' literary development of professional expertise, describing the 1945–46 achievement test in English composition as a test of writing ability developed "not only by practice in writing but also by the regular study of literature" (2). Texts that students were actually required to produce, however, were to feature the attributes of effective expository prose closely resembling the type of efficient language use that the board in 1931 had described as the particular need of the nonliterary student—notably clarity and logical structure. In the words of the 1945–46 *Bulletin of Information,* the test was intended to measure "the candidate's power to express ideas clearly and to organize them in a coherent form" (2).

Each of the three questions featured in the sample English Composition Achievement Test published in the bulletin for 1945–46 required students to produce a "well-planned paragraph" of approximately 150 words. The first question asked students to compare and contrast three paired sets of recreational activities:

> Write a paragraph of about 150 words stating the chief ways in which the forms of amusement in Column A below differ from those in Column B. Support your statement of the differences by a discussion which refers to the particular amusements listed.

A	B
Skating on a frozen pond	Watching a professional baseball game
Tracking rabbits; hikes to the mountains	A Sunday afternoon automobile ride in the country
Swimming in the millpond	Sandwiches and a portable radio on a modern bathing beach

Clearly the thought process students were to implement in order to respond to such a question is similar to that required by analogy items in the verbal SAT. They must first identify a relationship among the activities listed in each of the columns and then identify a relationship that distinguishes Column A from Column B. The logical structure of the resulting statement might be described as a ratio—for example, A : B as active : passive; or A : B as participant : spectator.

The instructions for the essay, moreover, require the discussion of these relationships to be structured according to the standard general-to-specific format of informative prose. Students are first to make a claim about the nature of the relationships they perceive among the activities listed and are then to provide explanatory support for that claim. Significantly, the directions make the explicit request that in supporting their claim, students make specific reference to the items on the list. The resulting paragraphs, then, are to be autonomous in the sense that the writer cannot assume the contents of the lists to be common knowledge shared by reader and writer. However true it may be that "we both know what is meant by Column A and Column B," students must not allow this assumption of shared knowledge to inform the structure or content of their paragraphs.

The second question likewise calls for students to engage in particular types of logical thinking—i.e., deduction and generalization—and to follow a general-to-specific format similar to that required in the first question. In this case, however, students are to support a claim by producing their own illustrations:

"A piece of stone may be to one person a paperweight; to another person it may be an unusual specimen of quartz."

In a paragraph of about 150 words explain what this sentence means and what it implies (i.e. what generalizations it fittingly supports). Provide two illustrations to support and make clear your explanation. (12)

The final question bears the closest resemblance of the three to the type of question typically featured in the prewar Comprehensive Examination in English. It requires students to reflect upon their reading background and to select a particularly instructive or otherwise meaningful reading experience. What distinguishes this question from the type often found in the Comprehensive Examination in English, however, is its specification that the student must select a nonfiction work for this discussion. Nonfiction works are then further defined by the sample categories listed—"a book, an essay, a magazine article, or an editorial in a newspaper" (12).

Students are furthermore instructed to treat the nonfiction work as a piece of informative-persuasive discourse, focusing on what the work has taught them and what the author has said to convince them of the topic's importance. A final note to students reminds them of the need for bibliographic information in academic discussions of another text: "At some appropriate point in your paragraph, give the name of the book, essay, magazine, or newspaper from which you have taken your material, and the author's name, if known" (12).

The College Board's *Bulletin of Information* for students preparing to take entrance exams for 1947–48 reveals that the English Composition Test could by that time include both essay and objective questions, and it provides examples of each type. The same statement of purpose that appeared in the previous bulletin is reprinted, emphasizing the development of a clear, well-organized prose style through writing practice and the study of literature. That year, however, the board was much more explicit about its scoring criteria, describing a rubric that analyzed effective academic writing into seven component skills: clarity of thought, organization of material, sentence structure, grammar, effectiveness and accuracy of vocabulary, punctuation, and spelling (7).

The sample test provided is composed of three sections, the first featuring multiple-choice questions to test mechanics and usage, the second requiring a 150-word paragraph in response to the same question about nonfiction reading that appeared on the 1945–46 sample exam, and the third asking students to revise a poorly written paragraph in order to improve its unity and coherence. The third section is of particular significance, since it anticipates the College Board's development of interlinear exercises, prominent in the English Composition Tests of the 1950s and the result of the board's efforts to strike a compromise between statisticians' demands for objective tests that could be reliably scored and English teachers' claims that writing ability could be assessed only if students actually produced written text.

The paragraph-revision task described in the 1947–48 bulletin features a prose paragraph about the three stages of Geoffrey Chaucer's literary career. Students are instructed to assume that the first and last sentences in the paragraph are acceptable as given, but intervening sentences require changes in diction, grammar, and sentence structure. "Such revision," the instructions go on to explain, "may involve some rearrangement of the order of your material. You must, however, retain all ideas presented in the paragraph and preserve its meaning completely." The autonomy of the text is even further emphasized by a closing comment that cautions the student, "Add no ideas of your own" (16).

By 1948, a wholly objective composition exam had replaced completely or partially essay-format exams of the immediately preceeding years. Those objective exams still maintained the intention of measuring clear, correct expression and the coherent organization of ideas, skills "normally developed in schools by practice in writing and by the study of literature" (CEEB *Bulletin of Information*, 1950, 28). Interestingly, however, the exams of that era required students to do no writing at all, and literary discourse was all but absent from the content of the exams.

Throughout the 1950s, the typical objective English Composition Test featured three multiple-choice sections that required students to identify and correct errors of grammar, mechanics, or usage; to describe grammar and usage errors in the language of English studies specialists (e.g., "lack of parallel construction," "faulty or ambiguous reference of pronoun"); and to complete short passages by supplying missing phrases from a selection of options. Alternatively, two multiple-choice sections could be featured, along with one interlinear exercise derived from paragraph-revision sections such as those appearing in composition tests between 1948 and 1951.

The interlinear item type is illustrated by part III of the English Composition Test that appears in the College Board's 1952–53 *Bulletin of Information* (29–30). Essentially, the exercise required students to edit a poorly written passage excerpted from a biographical essay about Henry James. Instead of rewriting the paragraph on a separate sheet of paper, however, as required by the paragraph-revision sections, students completed the interlinear exercise by employing a prescribed set of editorial marks to indicate changes they wanted to make. The text of the passage was formatted with wide spaces between the lines so students could make their corrections in the test booklet itself, a feature designed to facilitate efficient scoring.

The same interlinear sample exercise was repeated in the 1953–54 College Board bulletin, but by that time the directions had been augmented to make clear the connection perceived by the examiners between the interlinear exercise and the student's own composing process. The instruction, "You are to treat it [the biographical passage on Henry James] as though it were the first draft of a composition of your own" (33), no doubt indicates the extent to which the interlinear exercise was a concession to English teachers who complained that a wholly objective composition test was invalid because it did not engage students in the same activities they performed in actual composition. The sincerity of the board's claim that the interlinear exercise realistically approximated the revision stage of the composing process was cast into doubt, however, by further instructions that precluded the possibility that invention might occur during revision: "Do not omit any ideas and do not add any ideas of your own" (33).

The exclusion of invention from the skills and processes measured by objective composition exams was certainly not a new development, for pioneers in early scale measurements of writing ability had long ago recognized the impossibility of precisely measuring a nonmechanical skill such as invention. In 1917 Cross cited the difficulty in devising scales that could accurately measure aspects of writing "less mechanical" than, for instance, handwriting and spelling (185). Some years later, Steel and Talman (1936) aptly described the same dilemma in their justification of a scale designed to measure written expression divorced from considerations of content:

> There will be general agreement that composition ability is the ability to express oneself coherently, lucidly, and economically. We might argue on the ground that in valuating a composition the examiner has done all that he need do if he takes account of coherences and incoherences of expression, the lucidities and obscurities, the economies and wastes. But custom has decreed that the marker of composition shall attempt to valuate subject matter as well as the expression of it. . . .
>
> Nothing, we believe, has done more to make the marking of composition so notoriously unreliable. The only quality of subject-matter which can be assessed with any degree of reliability is the accuracy and the amount of information it conveys, and these must be regarded by the examiner of English composition as irrelevant to his immediate purpose. Some other qualities of subject-matter, such as its interest or its importance, cannot be measured objectively, for what is of interest and importance to one person is not necessarily of the same interest and importance to an-

other. . . . We conclude that the marker of compositions will mark all that he need mark if he valuates expression, that is, if he assesses the efficiency of the expression to communicate the ideas which shape it. (1–3)

Though Steel and Talman's experiments with writing assessment took place in Scotland, the problem with which they were grappling—the problem of unreliability in direct assessment of writing ability—was the same one that figured most prominently in the College Board's concerns at midcentury in this country. While Steel and Talman's solution to the problem of scoring unreliability was to simply disregard the elements of invention and content development in students' written responses to examination prompts, the College Board chose instead to eliminate those elements of composition altogether, in effect reducing composition to a fairly mechanical process that confronted the student only with decisions between right or wrong, appropriate or inappropriate choices.

Perhaps to offset the distinctly mechanical definition of literacy that was emerging from its purely objective composition tests during the fifties, the College Board evidently attempted to place more emphasis on literary discourse in those exams than it had done in the past. According to the College Board *Bulletin of Information,* the third part of the 1953–54 English Composition Test, for example, was designed to measure appreciation of style, tone, and meaning in short passages of poetry. The inclusion of such a section was justified, however, not as it might have been in years past when English departments themselves had more direct control over admissions standards in their area of expertise, by reference to the cultural importance of literary appreciation. Rather, the College Board bulletin explained, such an exercise had the more practical value of helping the student develop fundamental literacy skills. An "appreciation of style, tone, rhythm, and meaning" in poetic texts was not billed as a virtue in and of itself but was useful because "the ability to deal in a discriminating manner with such materials is closely related to abilities which the student must use in his own reading and writing" (34).

Exam items in this section present a brief poem with one line missing. Four possible versions of the missing line are then presented, from which the student must not only select the one that best completes the poem, but also identify the lines that are (1) inappropriate in rhythm and meaning, (2) inappropriate in style or tone, and (3) inappropriate in meaning. The following is a sample item of this type that appeared in the 1953-54 *Bulletin of Information* (34).

> Silence in love suggests more woe
> Than words, though ne'er so witty:
> A beggar that is dumb, you know,

a. Will ne'er win love or pity.
b. Gets, God knows, lots of pity.
c. May demand of us extra pity.
d. May challenge double pity.

The College Board's English Composition Test retained its three-part objective format for some time. Although English studies specialists themselves continued to challenge the validity of a composition test that involved students in no actual composition, statisticians argued for the validity of objective composition tests on the basis of their predictive success. In 1954, Huddleston published an influential study finding objective measures of English studies skills (the verbal SAT and an objective editing test) to be more valid predictors of academic success in English than essay composition exams. Huddleston used as her criteria college English grades and "systematic ratings of writing ability by teachers who knew the students well" (qtd. in Godshalk et al. 2).

The results of studies such as these provided a sufficient rationale for the board's continued reliance on objective composition measures, although between 1954 and 1971 a number of concessions were made to educators who insisted on some form of direct assessment. Between 1954 and 1956, for instance, a two-hour all-essay General Composition Test was offered once a year as an alternative to the English Composition Test. Focusing on topics defined as "general problems of wide interest," the General Composition Test provided students with reading materials to supply background information on the topic. After reading the materials, followed by an essay prompt in the form of a question, students were to prepare an outline, write an essay, and summarize the theme of the essay. According to the *Bulletin of Information* for 1954–55, topics that were actually used in the exam were "Should women be given the same educational and professional opportunities as men?" and "Is there a conflict between science and human values?" (35).

The essay responses to the exam questions were scored according to an analytic rather than a holistic approach. The five qualities on which the essays were to be judged were mechanics, style, organization, reasoning, and content. Instructions to the students taking the exam defined those qualities as follows:

> Mechanics—Your ability to use correct forms of grammar, to punctuate, and to spell correctly
>
> Style—Your ability to state your ideas clearly and effectively in language which is appropriate to your essay
>
> Organization—Your ability to arrange the parts of your essay in such a way as to make your ideas and purposes clear to your readers
>
> Reasoning—Your ability to support your conclusions with evidence and to reason in such a way as to convince your readers of the soundness of your conclusions
>
> Content—Your ability to supplement the reading materials given with materials drawn from your general reading, your school studies, and your own life (35)

Examinees were reassured that "your essay will be judged impartially by qualified readers," though no explanation is provided as to what the readers' qualifications might be. The alleged impartiality of the readers likewise opens up some questions. If an impartial judgment is one that disregards the point of view chosen by the writer, or that fails to evaluate the writer's moral or ethical position, focusing instead on only the formal qualities of argumentative discourse, then the General Composition Test is little different from the other College Board tests discussed in this chapter. It projects the same definition of academic literacy that coincides with Olson's description of "essayist technique," emphasizing the creation of an autonomous expository text, structured according to conventions of academic language and formal logic rather than the shared knowledge, experience, or affective disposition of reader and writer. And, of course, as is virtually inevitable in an assessment context, formal properties of the text are more important than functional, or transactional, success. Adhering to conventional forms of language and argumentation contributes more to the "success" of the text than does the text's ability to persuade or inform an intended audience.

The Persistence of Formalism in Academic Definitions of Literacy

Examinations, by their very nature, tend to focus on the products rather than the processes of literacy. If the examination is intended as a measure of reading, for instance, it very likely attempts to assess the knowledge or information the examinee has retained from a brief reading exercise or from a more extensive reading preparation. Similarly, if the exam is a measure of writing ability, it usually involves examiners evaluating a finished product or, in the case of objective composition exams, specific information students have supplied to indicate their knowledge of written language conventions. To the extent that examiners generally assess literate ability and behavior only on the basis of artifacts of that ability and behavior, their concerns may be said to be primarily formal as opposed to functional. By the very nature of their enterprise, examiners are more concerned with the examinees' ability to produce the acceptable form of a written communication effort than they are with their communicative intentions or their success in effectively communicating an intended meaning to an intended audience.

Additionally, we must acknowledge that the emphasis on form over communicative function is reinforced by the testing situation itself. Although, as I pointed out in chapter 5, essay prompts including information about hypothetical rhetorical situations began to appear in English entrance exams during the early twentieth century, test instructions to students have rarely if ever formally acknowledged the real rhetorical situation that encompasses the writing and reading of English studies examinations. In fact, recent efforts on the part of test makers to present texts as autonomous receptacles of meaning and to remain uninvolved in a communicative exchange by disavowing any necessary adherence to the value systems expressed in reading passages seemingly indicate to students that functional communication is a nonessential component of the literacy skills allegedly measured by such tests. A similar effect is achieved by instructions assuring students that their essays will be read by impartial readers and admonishing them not to call upon any prior knowledge they may have in connection with the substance of reading passages in the test.

Such stipulations characterize reading and writing as a predominantly formal, as opposed to functional, activity and in doing so violate the terms most essential to language use as it is currently described by leading theorists and pedagogues. As W. Ross Winterowd has insisted, language, whether written or spoken, cannot exist without meaning. His claim, in turn, points to the difficult question of just where linguistic meaning resides. As the poststructuralist and reader-response critics who have ascended in the modern English literary studies profession insist and as the process model of composition instruction assumes, it is an oversimplification—in fact, a distortion—of literate activity to claim that meaning can simply reside in the text, uninfluenced by the situational and historical context in which the text was produced or read. Winterowd explains this point to his own readers by observing,

> You're reading a book right now. Is the meaning "in" the book, to be extracted like gold nuggets from a mine, or is it elsewhere? To continue the metaphor: as a reader, are you like a miner, digging out the meaning contained in the book? Or are you more like a cabinet maker, using the materials afforded by the book to construct a meaning?
> A bit of reflection will convince you, I think, that readers are cabinet makers, not miners. To get right to the point, meaning is not "down there" on the page, but potentially "up here" in your mind. The text enables you to construct the meaning. (58)

While Winterowd's conception of literacy in these lines is informed by theories current in both literature and composition studies, the two branches into which this history has described the division of English studies' professional product, it obviously conflicts in fundamental ways with the definition of literacy promoted by modern standardized testing methods. As we have seen, the disjunction between the discipline's sense of its professional product and the product as it is defined by external authorities is in large part due to the process of centralization that has progressively characterized educational developments since the First World War. When that process absorbed the movement to standardize college entrance examinations, a movement initiated by English studies specialists representing individual colleges and secondary schools, it signaled a certain loss of professional autonomy for the discipline. As I have pointed out elsewhere in this chapter, English studies professionals staged a long resistance to what amounted to a bureaucratic usurpation of their right to define their professional products and services and to set standards of inclusion and exclusion to their ranks. In the end, however, bureaucratization imposed its inevitable consequences.

Foremost among the consequences was the pattern of compartmentalization brought to bear upon the definition of literacy as a professional product. Particularly noticeable in this regard is the division of reading and writing into separate and only tenuously related areas of professional expertise. Once the separation was entrenched, the two major branches of English studies came increasingly to be identified within the profession itself with the two conflicting ideological currents that have complicated the development of English studies since its appearance as a modern academic profession during the nineteenth century. On the one hand reading rose from the foundation of literary studies that English inherited from the classical text-based curriculum. Along with the inheritance of a particular educational format came the motive of cultural leadership and the belief that higher education existed for the purpose of preserving high culture and producing cultural leaders. Writing, or composition, on the other hand, has associated itself more freely with the utilitarian philosophy that distinguishes the modern university from its classical ancestry.

The compartmentalization of literacy has been absorbed by the professionalization process in such a way that writing, institutionalized as composition studies, has become largely associated with the public service mandate that is essential to the health and prosperity of any profession. Reading, institutionalized as literary studies and more recently as critical studies, meanwhile, has taken on much of the representation of the "special," or "arcane," knowledge that sets the profession apart from potential market competitors.

As we have seen, one particular configuration of the specialized knowledge that in its most exemplary form transcends instruction is literary appreciation, defined as an untutored sensitivity to the aesthetic and cultural values embedded in texts. By virtue of its exemption from instruction and measurement, this strand of professional knowledge making has remained more securely based within the profession itself and has been far less subject to external definition than its service-oriented counterpart in composition studies. Accordingly, the more "basic" forms of literacy that typically find a home in the rhetoric and composition branch of English studies are subject to definition as "verbal scholastic aptitude," whereas the reading of literary texts continues to maintain a unique departmental association and as such undergoes measurement and institutional definition as "achievement" within a specialized subject area.

In chapter 7, I will examine more closely how the compartmentalization of literacy as a professional knowledge base has been enforced by examination formats and how entrance exams have been administered. From there I will proceed to speculate upon the consequences that current testing practices predict for the professional status of English studies and their implications for the criteria against which literacy, as the essential product of education in this country, will be measured.

CHAPTER SEVEN

Administrative Control of Academic Literacy

Content of the Verbal SAT

In 1947, the College Board joined forces with the Carnegie Foundation and the National Education Association in forming the Educational Testing Service (ETS), a separate and centralized administrative agency that would carry out the board's testing responsibilities. The founding of ETS signaled a transformation in the collective personality of those involved in developing and scoring entrance examinations. As we have seen, the original College Board consisted of college faculty members and secondary school teachers representing individual academic departments. Initially it was that collection of instructors who collaborated in designing and administering the examinations in their own subject divisions. As the auspices of the College Board expanded, however, and as the technology involved in educational testing advanced, much of the control over entrance examinations passed from the hands of instructors into the hands of administrators and psychometricians who had the expertise required for the successful running of so large and scientifically oriented an operation. As chapter 6 suggested, an immediate consequence of those developments for the field of English studies has been the surrender of a certain degree of professional autonomy, particularly in formulating a definition of the most service-oriented branch of the profession's knowledge base.

By the end of the First World War, the vocational bent of the modern academy was firmly entrenched. English studies, with a heritage rooted in the liberal tradition, found itself increasingly displaced from the center of the curriculum and more and more called into the service of other academic areas of specialization. Vernacular literacy was still very much central to intellectual productivity in the academy as a whole, but as the unique province of English departments it was increasingly receptive to definition by external demands. The most influential of those demands came from academic departments that enjoyed more direct connections with the interests of federal and corporate funding agencies. As a professional entity, English studies responded to the ascendance of those departments by developing programs for instruction in technical and business writing and, more recently, has taken charge of such enterprises as writing-across-the-curriculum and English as a Second Language.

To compensate for the loss of autonomy implied by such developments, English studies has tended to center its professional identity in the text-based province of critical reading. Initially dominated by an interest in the aesthetic form of literary texts that represent cultural preeminence, this facet of the profession has lately come to focus more upon the function of texts as indicators and transmitters of culture. Through such permutations, however, the traditional value of literacy as a prerequisite to cultural leadership has been upheld: the capacity to read culture and to understand its production is essentially the potential to exercise some degree of control over cultural production.

In keeping with the differential positioning of reading and writing within the professional domain of English studies, entrance examinations that govern the reading and comprehension of literary texts are currently conceived as optional achievement tests whose content is specifically linked to the dominant professional knowledge base of English studies. The more "basic" literacy skills and abilities, which are likely to be advanced in English department courses with labels like "composition and rhetoric," are diffused into the general category of "verbal scholastic aptitude" and as such are assessed in what can roughly be described as a cross-curricular format administered by an essentially nonacademic entity. In order to more fully comprehend the implications of such developments, it is worthwhile at this point to examine the SAT itself in further detail, paying particular attention to the definition of academic literacy implicit in an exam that is thus described as "curriculum free" and that, moreover, is "read" by computerized scoring procedures.

The Curriculum-Free Content of the Verbal SAT

The issue of the SAT verbal examination's subject matter has been controversial for many years (see Owen, *None of the Above*; Nairn et al.). In theory, the SAT is a curriculum-free exam which requires no specific preparatory course work. But in actual practice, the test attempts to embrace a broadly conceived notion of curricular knowledge. No test featuring language use can ever truly be devoid of content that can be described as subject matter, since as representational symbols, words necessarily signify content of one kind or another. With the possible exception of the artificial language items, discontinued in 1927 after only one year of use, all of the SAT verbal items involve some vocabulary knowledge. Chances of successfully responding to the vocabulary items are greatly improved for those examinees who have some familiarity with the meanings of the featured words.

Analogy questions, for instance, are designed to measure a certain type of knowledge-acquisition skill—associational reasoning ability (Donlan 46). But in an analogy question such as the 1943 item (day : night = intrepidity : ?), students may well understand the relationship of simple opposition between day and night and still fail to answer the question correctly because of insufficient vocabulary knowledge. Associational reasoning cannot come into play, in other words, if students do not know the meaning of "intrepidity" or of the various other Latinate terms comprising their response alternatives: "pusillaminity," "benevolence," "restitution," and "simony."

College Board historian Loret reported in 1960 that the early forms of the SAT verbal section emphasized content areas that were well in line with a traditional liberal arts preparatory curriculum. Reading passages tended to feature aesthetic-philosophical topics as well as topics concerning human relationships, and vocabulary items were such as students might be expected to encounter in preparatory reading in literature, philosophy, and history. In the course of years, however, the content areas of the exam began to reflect the modernization of the curriculum by including subject matter drawn from scientific studies as well as current political events and contemporary life. As Loret explains, between 1930 and 1960, the College Board paid increased attention to the issue of content, and viewed collectively, the SAT verbal sections administered during that time demonstrate a trend away from "essentially random content sampling" to "carefully stratified content sampling" (20). By 1960, test developers were attempting to create vocabulary tests that provided equal emphasis on the content of four specified areas: "aesthetic-philosophical," "human relationships," "scientific world," and "world of practical affairs."

Similarly, by 1960, reading-comprehension sections of the SAT, according to College Board policy, were to draw systematically from content supplied by four recognized academic disciplinary divisions: biological sciences, physical sciences, humanities, and social studies. The passages drawn from those areas, moreover, were to provide a fairly equal sampling of three discourse modes: narration, exposition, and argumentation (Loret 21). In 1984 Donlan listed the same content categories that Loret described in 1960 but admitted that the categories themselves frequently overlap and are difficult to adhere to. "Inevitably," he writes, "they suggest a correspondence with subject categories that doesn't exist" (47). In addition to the four content categories, reading-comprehension items as of 1984 have included two modal categories: narration and argumentative discourse. According to Donlan, the narrative passages are excerpted from works of fiction, while the argumentative passages are usually propaganda or polemical material (47).

It is difficult to say with certainty whether the College Board has adhered to its stated policy regarding content in the SAT verbal test throughout the past quarter century. For security reasons, SAT's that have actually been administered are not made available to the public, and sample items published in issues of the CEEB *Bulletin of Information* or, more recently, in pamphlets entitled *Taking the SAT* in order to help students prepare for the exam are so limited in number that they provide little evidence of actual subject-matter frequency and distribution in the tests. In 1980, however, the passage of New York's disclosure law required testing agencies such as the College Board to make copies of test questions and answers as well as the students' own answer sheets available to students who had taken testing-agency exams. In response to the ruling the College Board decided to publish in book form a collection of previously administered SAT's for prospective college applicants to use as study guides to familiarize themselves with the exam's format and the range of questions and topics that might appear on an SAT exam.

To the extent that the sample items included in the ten SAT's published by the College Board in 1986 accurately represent the frequency with which the four subject divisions appear in reading-comprehension passages, this particular collection perhaps indicates a slight bias toward the traditional liberal arts curriculum. Of sixty passages presented in the 1986 edition of *Ten SAT's*, seventeen seem to qualify as humanities subject matter, thirteen as social sciences, twelve as biological sciences, and ten as physical sciences. An additional eight passages were drawn from fictional works. This count is admittedly an unreliable indicator, however, since *10 SAT's* contains only a sampling of test items. Furthermore, the reading passages included in the collection demonstrate a considerable overlap among the four disciplinary divisions. At least two passages, for instance, discuss the history of scientific methodology. Such passages feature subject matter drawn from both physical and biological sciences and also include information about history and philosophy. Should the passages, then, be categorized as biological science, physical science, or humanities readings?

The interdisciplinary content of SAT reading passages, along with the SAT's emphasis on formal logic, contributes to a modern definition of academic literacy that departs markedly from that which informed the achievement tests in English during the late nineteenth and early twentieth centuries. Although those essay-type exams required students to possess a type of literacy that enabled them to demonstrate a familiarity with prescribed literary texts and an appreciative understanding of the cultural ideals conveyed by the texts, the verbal SAT has progressively minimized literary study, focusing instead on comprehension of the logical structure of texts. Even when literary passages are included in the reading-comprehension sections of the SAT, their presentation seems to highlight logical structure. An excerpt from *Middlemarch* included in Form Code 4X of the 1986 *10 SAT's,* for instance, reveals Mr. Casaubon's thoughts about his and Dorothea's courtship. The questions that follow require students to identify both the definition of courtship implicit in Mr. Casaubon's reasoning and Mr. Casaubon's primary reason for desiring marriage. Finally, students are asked to select from four alternatives the best summary of Casaubon's rationale for his disappointment with courtship (294).

Reading ability, as a component of literacy reflected by the SAT, then, has come to be viewed as an interdisciplinary skill. Not only have test makers sought to liberate reading from a specific preparatory English curriculum, they have also attempted to generalize it beyond the established content boundaries of the English studies discipline. Consequently, skill in certain "mental operations" has come to constitute academic literacy as it is measured by most college entrance examination procedures.

On the surface, such developments seem to remove even the reading aspect of literacy from the exclusive professional terrain of English studies, making it, instead, the shared province of many academic disciplines. For the most part, however, pedagogical realities contradict the assumption that a variety of disciplines view the production of literacy skills as a part of their professional mandates. At the college level, writing-across-the-curriculum movements are far more visible than gestures toward reading-across-the-curriculum. To be sure, we are now seeing increased textbook offerings in across-the- curriculum readers, typically featuring prose articles from disciplinary divisions strikingly familiar to those articulated by SAT test makers. But in practice, such readers are nearly always marketed exclusively to English department personnel. In terms of English studies' professional expertise, the market conditions supported by the forms and procedures of standardized entrance testing reinforce the notion that English studies is, at least in part, a "service" department whose product must meet the demands of a clientele beyond itself.

That service function, as we have seen, is essential to the growth and survival of all professions, and English studies has long identified its own service function as twofold: ministering to literacy crises that threaten to render individuals less effective as citizens in a democracy and, on a loftier level, shaping and preserving cultural standards. With the official appearance of scholastic aptitude in the 1926 exam, however, it became apparent that the clientele of the English studies profession had shifted substantially. Because academic literacy as an entrance requirement was by that point so closely equated with general scholastic aptitude, and only incidentally with cultural concerns outside of academic life, English studies then found it necessary and expedient to market its product primarily to entities within the academic bureaucracy rather than to the public at large. Students needed to read and write well not because, in any direct and immediate sense, these abilities made them better, more responsible citizens, but because reading and writing well could make them more effective students in a curriculum growing ever more vocational and ever more absorbed by its credentialing function.

Indirectly, of course, service to other academic departments can still be viewed as service to the general populace. Seen from the perspective of national economic and political interests, if English studies can help business and engineering departments turn out more capable managers and engineers, then the nation as a whole is well served. On the other hand, to come under the employ of professional colleagues in other academic departments signals some loss in professional autonomy and status. We may speculate that such developments are the long-term result of English studies' once-cherished belief that the schooled individual who can read and write possesses superior intellect as well as superior education. Because of that widely held conviction, Crossley, author of the 1916 report on the causes of failure in college, apparently felt no need to explain or support his claim that "family illiteracy" and "intellectual inheritance" are one and the same. Nor did Willard Uhl, spokesman for the NCTE's Philological Council, hesitate to publicize in 1927 the reported high correlation between "general mental ability" and results obtained from reading tests. Uhl summed up the significance of this finding with the remark, "One may conclude that intelligence scores are a significant indication of ability in English" (53).

With the advent of intelligence tests in the early twentieth century, however, came "scientific" validation of such beliefs as well as the threatening prospect of their appropriation by the scientific community. Largely composed of verbal items, early intelligence tests provided a model for the development of a scholastic aptitude test that could predict with a high degree of reliability a student's performance not only in college English courses but in higher education in general. While the development of the Scholastic Aptitude Test as an eventual replacement for the traditional achievement tests in various academic disciplines was an important step toward institutionally generalizing academic literacy beyond the disciplinary confines of English studies, the inclination to broaden the accepted definition of academic literacy had already been initiated by the willingness of many schools and the College Board itself to accommodate nonliterary students' claims to the right of higher education. Because increasing numbers of these students were bound for relatively new and heavily funded vocational programs such as business and the various applied sciences, the literacy standards of a strictly liberal arts program had grown conspicuously inadequate for predicting college performance. The SAT, because it was a single test that purportedly measured a curriculum-free, general scholastic ability, became a convenient basis for decisions about an unprecedentedly broad range of college applicants. In the process of assuming that role, the SAT records a new stage in the competitive strategies of English studies in the professional marketplace, a stage that conforms to Barrow's hypothesis that the mission of higher education in this country has, over the course of the twentieth century, been increasingly dictated by competition for the material means to support knowledge production—the federal, foundational, and corporate grants and contracts that can support academic labor in ways academic salaries cannot.

Computer Technology and an Analytic Approach to Literacy: The Medium Is the Message

Building upon an implicit definition of reading ability as accumulated conventionalized knowledge about the medium of written language and the construction of academic texts, tests like the SAT take an analytic approach to the measurement of literacy by dividing written language into discreet component parts and by dividing the cognitive processes involved in reading and writing into a limited number of "mental operations." Donlan illustrates the presumed connection between item types and cognitive operations with the examples of antonyms and analogues, which require "associational reasoning," and sentence-completion and reading-comprehension items, which require "ability to infer meaning and logical relationships from context" (46). Within the category of reading-comprehension items, moreover, the board has identified six subcategories of questions, each type intended to test a different component of reading skill. Two of the categories are described as "basic comprehension questions," and the skills they measure are (1) "the comprehension of the main idea as explicitly stated" and (2) "the comprehension of a supporting idea as explicitly stated." Three other categories emphasize logical reasoning skills involved in the following tasks: (3)

"the completion of an intended inference," (4) "the application of some principle stated in the passage to a hypothetical case," and (5) "the evaluation of the logic of the language in the passage." The final skills category tested is described as (6) "sensitivity to various aspects of language," represented by "the perception of the style and tone of the passage" (Donlan 48).

To a large extent, as I have argued earlier, this analytic approach was encouraged by the academic community's growing respect for scientific method, an ideology paralleled by the growth of the applied sciences in strength and number within a college curriculum formerly dominated by the liberal arts. As Tuman has maintained, English studies, with its professional knowledge base that privileges poetic, nonreferential truth, has always been particularly susceptible to this sort of peer pressure from its more conspicuously utilitarian and empirically based departmental colleagues:

> English as an academic discipline . . . has always been inse-
> cure with its own understanding of truth, has always been
> too eager to be accepted by those disciplines whose concept
> of truth is grounded in the methodology of the natural sci-
> ences, and thus has always been too deferential to the
> claims of positivism. Yielding to these historical pressures,
> English professors have tended to see the reading of literary
> texts either as a source of a special knowledge unique to a
> narrow range of aesthetic experience . . . or as a healthy di-
> version from our relentless search for explanations of all
> experience, cultural as well as natural, that will attain the
> universality, the objectivity, and the ahistoricity of the natu-
> ral sciences. (*Preface* 61–62)

Additional reinforcement of the analytic approach, however, came from the emergence of computer technology during the 1950s. Not only did this new technology make it possible for standardized testing agencies such as ETS to meet corporate standards of efficiency and cost-effectiveness in processing the entrance examinations of unprece-dented numbers of applicants, but it also made possible the produc-tion of composite test scores based upon large numbers of subscores, each of which in turn derived from large numbers of individual-item scores. Computers, in short, made the task of analysis—in particular, statistical analysis—infinitely easier and possible at vastly more complex levels than had previously been the case.

But it is not only in their accommodation of a certain type of examination format that computers have been influential in the formulation of a late-twentieth-century definition of academic literacy. We might also say that computer technology has provided a new metaphor for describing the human mind. With the advent of artificial intelligence it became possible to conceive of the human brain as an information-processing mechanism—a construct that has figured prominently in a great deal of reading and writing research in recent decades. The computer metaphor, in fact, is embedded in the formal literacy theories of such scholars as Havelock, Ong, Olson, and Goody and Watt, all of whom argue that literacy facilitated a cognitive change in the human mind because written texts, constituting the potential of an almost infinite measure of information storage *outside* the human brain, freed portions of the brain formerly devoted to the function of memory, or information storage, to engage in other cognitive operations. The basic assumption here is that the human mind is composed of "data banks" that take up work space that might otherwise contribute to an expanded "active file."

Nor is it only in the realm of historical studies of literacy and its cognitive consequences that the computer metaphor is invoked in formulating theories about how the human mind functions during the processes of reading and writing. Studies by cognitive researchers into literacy commonly use terminology drawn from the field of computer science to label cognitive activities and sites or processes in the brain that are activated during literacy events. The resultant theories of literacy, based on the premise that artificial intelligence provides a model for explaining natural human intelligence, obviously fit well with literacy testing methods that construe literacy as a complex of cognitive operations or behaviors that may be isolated and measured separately from one another.

Consider, for example, Linda Flower and John Hayes's proposal of a cognitive-process theory of composing (1981). They describe their task as the need to "define the major elements or sub-processes that make up the larger process of writing" and to "show how these various elements of the process interact with the total process of writing" (368). In their investigation of these subprocesses, Flower and Hayes analyze thinking-aloud protocols of their subjects and identify hierarchically organized "subroutines"—such as retrieving information from long-term memory—that writers use in producing texts. All of these subroutines are under the surveillance of a "monitor," a mechanism supervising the writer's switching from one subroutine to another. Articulated in terms such as "human information processing systems," "executive control," "feedback loop," and "surveillance mechanisms," versions of the computer model of human intelligence are obviously adaptable to computerized literacy testing methods and to a mechanized view of literacy itself. Unfortunately, however, the requirements of literacy testing formats and procedures based upon that, as any, model are necessarily limited to describing and "making count" only those features of literacy that the model is capable of revealing. And a significant shortcoming of the computer model is that it can account for literacy only in formal terms. In his diatribe against a "strict cognitivist" approach to literacy, David Dobrin calls upon Searle's "Chinese Room Argument" to point up the failures of a formalist approach to reading and writing. Searle's conceit features a man who has no functional knowledge of Chinese. The man is placed in a room where he consults a book of rules in order to produce correct responses, in Chinese, to questions presented to him in Chinese. While the rule book enables the man to answer the questions correctly and thus to accurately simulate what a real Chinese person would do in his situation, the man has no understanding of the Chinese symbols he is manipulating. Dobrin comments upon this hypothetical scene with the following:

> What does a Chinese person have that the little-man-in-the-room does not? Essentially, in understanding Chinese, the Chinese person's mental states *represent* or are about something outside the states themselves. The man-in-the-room's responses, on the other hand, do not represent. They are not about anything. This ability to represent is the irreducibly mental aspect of the mental. Computational states, which consist of formal counters (meaningless symbols manipulated by formal rules), have only formal relationships with other counters. None of these represent anything. (70)

The computer, in other words, cannot account for anything outside the rule-governed system in which it operates. Like objective tests of writing, then, the computer model of human intelligence inadequately accounts for skills and processes that do not conform to formal literacy theory because they are not obviously rule governed. It is for this reason that cognitive psychologists Marlena Scardamalia and Carl Bereiter, in their study of cognitive processes involved in composing, acknowledge the same inability to speak to the question of invention that plagued the early developers of scale measurements (see, for example, Cross's 1917 article). Discussing a figure that illustrates a process pattern they have observed in children's composing processes, they concede their inability to explain how writers initiate the pattern in the first place: "Figure 1 does not show how the process starts, how the initial comparison between written and intended text is instigated. That is a matter of considerable uncertainty and one that is bypassed in the present investigation by using a facilitating procedure that automatically starts the process" (5).

Criticism of modern educational research techniques and procedures, such as computer-based models of human cognition and the kinds of objective tests with which such models seem to exist in a relationship of mutual reinforcement, tends to come from humanists who, as we have discovered, have historically insisted upon their own brand of formalism. (A well-known contemporary proponent of formal humanism is E. D. Hirsch, whose concept of cultural literacy is based upon the premise that knowledge of certain texts and other codified forms of knowledge together constitute a culturally literate individual.) These critics point out that these techniques support a mechanical conception of literacy in many ways antithetical to the liberal tradition from which the English version of academic literacy was born. Such a conception highlights the notion of isolated component skills while deemphasizing transactional aspects of literate activity, such as social context, communicative intent, and the creation and exchange of meaning.

This mechanized construction of literacy in the form of objective and computer-scored exams is in many ways the logical result of the standardization process that characterizes the history of college entrance examinations in this country. As the years have passed, the exams have tended more and more to represent the examinee in terms that bear obvious similarities to those describing the situation of the man in the Chinese room. We can observe, for example, an increasing tendency throughout the history of English entrance examinations to isolate the examinee's reading and writing activities from any genuine rhetorical context. Although the very earliest essay exams provided no explicit information about the actual purpose and audience for which the examinee was writing, the narrowly limited reading list and the fairly homogeneous nature of the academic community at that time indirectly provided considerable information about the rhetorical parameters of the testing situation. Moreover, the preparatory school's deliberate focus on grooming students to write successful essays for the college entrance examinations served as a sort of academic apprenticeship enabling students to acquire essential local knowledge about the academic discourse community they sought to enter. By the time preparatory students took their entrance examinations, they had accumulated a good bit of practice in writing according to the discourse conventions of that community. And, as Michael Carter has recently pointed out, from such accumulated local experience comes expertise. "Expertise is founded on local knowledge," Carter writes. "Experts are successful in their fields because they bring to their performance domain-specific knowledge attained through much experience within that domain" (269).

Because questions on the early exams typically required the recall of factual information, they fell into the category Arons and Lawrence refer to as Type I, "Do you know what I know?" (241). Based upon a short reading list that had to a large extent been the focus of the students' preparatory studies, such questions implied the common knowledge of subject matter that united student writers and their readers and contributed to structuring the specific domain in which students formulated their responses. As the lists grew more extensive and less prescriptive, however, and as secondary education became less exclusively focused on preparation for the college entrance exam, students encountered the exams with less certainty concerning the rhetorical dimensions of their performance.

As standardization of examinations spread as a result of the College Entrance Examination Board's growth as a centralized testing agency, the rhetorical situation controlling entrance examination procedures became even more diffuse. The audience for whom examinees wrote their essays was more distant, more anonymous than in the days when students wrote their entrance exams on site at the particular colleges to which they were applying, often in the presence of the very person or persons who would read and evaluate what they had written. This alienation of writer from reader in the testing situation grew progressively during the era of objective tests, when scoring became a mechanical task that could be carried out by unskilled workers who were often entirely unfamiliar with the test itself. Finally, as computer technology came of age in the field of educational assessment and as questions called for less and less actual reading and writing, demanding only indirect evidence of literate abilities, students taking entrance exams were literally directing their communications to a machine.

Pedagogical Consequences of Current Standardized Literacy Testing

In a variety of ways the mechanization of literacy testing has contributed immeasurably to an increasingly mechanical notion of academic literacy itself, as technological production stamps its imprint on this "essential product" of schooling. In much of the cognitivist rhetoric surrounding the subject of academic literacy, the same machines that are used to measure literacy skills via objective examinations are also frequently invoked as the models that can explain literacy as a set of cognitive operations. Although the machine-scored measures of literacy achieve much greater reliability than previous tests, they tend to focus exclusively on fairly rigid, rule-governed or mechanical aspects of literacy while discounting more creative and locally governed aspects such as invention or integration of textually conveyed information with prior knowledge and direct experience.

The emphasis on general, rule-governed features of literacy in an effort to establish the empirical credibility of testing, however, implies some disturbing consequences for literacy education. Mischler, for example, maintains that current educational research and pedagogy tend to ignore the importance of social context and local constraints to the task of knowledge construction because of their eagerness to embrace the privileged epistemic of scientific inquiry. Citing IQ tests and their variants as examples of the tendency to strip away context in an effort to establish universal, context-free laws of human behavior, Mischler argues that the positivist model from which such methods derive seriously distorts the behavior allegedly being observed. Kretovics is similarly critical of the empirical bias of current educational research and pedagogy. Mainstream institutionalized education, he observes, attempts to divorce its activities from a social context by espousing "the logic of objectivity and neutrality" that identifies education as a "neutral and autonomous institution" (51–52).

Particularly troublesome to educational critics such as Mischler and Kretovics is the extent to which the alleged neutrality and universality of educational principles discourage students and educators from exploring the critical and creative potentials of literacy. Endorsing a functional approach to literacy education that closely resembles Freire's pedagogy, they argue separately that academically instilled literacy should lead students, first of all, to perceive relationships between themselves and school, and between school and the social context in which it exists. Secondly, they maintain, literacy that is taught in the schools should encourage students to reflect critically upon those relationships and, perhaps, to formulate alternative educational practices that can alter their own destinies as well as education's position in society (Kretovics 53–54).

With particular respect to English studies, a number of scholars have charged that the mechanization of literacy within the academic community, largely through the agency of standardized objective tests such as the SAT, enforces a notion of literacy devoid of meaningful purpose because it occurs within a communicative vacuum. Prominent among such charges is the claim that tests such as the SAT perpetuate a preparatory language arts curriculum that places more emphasis on "busy work" than on meaningful literate activity that takes place within a communicative context. Owen, who spent the winter of 1979 posing as a senior in a large public high school in Stratford, Connecticut, for instance, writes of the ways he believes the influence of tests such as the SAT discourage substantial reading and writing experience in the high school classroom:

> In English class we spent six weeks reading a 55-page book and devoted most of the rest of our time to memorizing

lists of vocabulary words and solving SAT-like multiple-choice brainteasers: antonyms, analogies, sentence completions. We almost never had to write anything and, aside from our weekly 10-page assignments, we didn't have to read. In large measure our time was spent doing multiple-choice busywork. One of the reasons for this, I think, is that over the years ETS has made busywork seem like real work. With its PSATs, SATs, GREs, GMATs, LSATs and dozens of other tests, the company has given the multiple-choice question a pedagogic credibility it does not deserve.

That is not to suggest that teachers would immediately start assigning papers if ETS disappeared. But as school budgets have declined, ETS has given teachers an easy rationalization for abandoning time-consuming assignments. If multiple-choice questions are good enough for an exalted national testing program, they must be good enough for English 12. As long as the tests provide, or seem to provide, the standard by which society's rewards are allocated, schools will inevitably remake themselves in the image of the tests. When this transformation also lightens the loads of overworked teachers, it takes place all the more quickly. (*The SAT and Social Stratification* 90–91)

Even standardized test makers themselves are aware of the influence their instruments may exert in the classroom and, by extension, on society at large. In the years following the College Board's introduction of the objective SAT in 1926, educational researchers have reported steadily increasing use of similarly "objective" varieties of educational materials and classroom activities. The College Board's Advisory Panel on the Scholastic Aptitude Test Score Decline, for instance, reported in 1977 the burgeoning use of activities such as underlining, circling, fill-in-the-blanks, and single-word written answers in elementary and secondary schools, usually at the expense of sustained writing practice (cited in Ravitch).

Responding to this report, Diane Ravitch has maintained that the SAT itself has not *caused* these practices but acknowledges that "the curriculum-free SAT has presented no impediment" to curricular and pedagogical revisions whose effects have undermined certain desirable educational standards, particularly those used to define literacy in the academy:

When these busywork activities are substituted for student writing, they are anti-intellectual and subversive of good learning. Filling-in-the-blanks is not equivalent educationally to the intellectual task involved in writing an essay, in which the student must think through what he wants to say, must organize his thoughts, must choose his words with care, and must present his thoughts with precision. (26)

The mounting intensity of such criticisms in recent years lies behind the College Board's efforts through ETS in 1989 to revise their format in order to include direct-assessment portions in their measurement of verbal skills. In light of such recognitions that testing methods, particularly college entrance testing methods, affect classroom activities and educational philosophies, we must acknowledge a certain irony in charges leveled against the academic community for failing to provide students with adequate literacy skills when those charges are overwhelmingly based upon the evidence of declining test scores. Conceivably what is happening is that the tests being used are able to *predict* academic success, but are not equally capable of *promoting* that success. Moreover, as a number of critics have observed, predictive measures such as the SAT actually erect a barrier to the educational reforms that the widespread alarm of "Johnny can't read" seems to demand. The College Board's Commission on Tests, for instance, reported in 1974 that the tests in the board's Admissions Testing Program are antithetical to progressive education because their predictive nature reinforces an inclination to maintain the status quo. Their validity, after all, results from their power to predict who will and who will not succeed in the educational system as it currently exists. If the system should change radically from within, the definitive power of standardized testing would be fatally undermined.

The conservative effects of such tests are most immediately felt at selective colleges where test scores are an important criterion for admission, the commission writes, but they also extend to other institutions that derive their ideas about educational standards from the example set by the selective schools. Consequently, the commission notes, the conservative influence of current testing methods is virtually universal in this country:

Thus highly selective colleges reject students whose particular configuration of talents does not make them easy to instruct successfully by classic methods in traditional subjects, and less selective colleges emulate them insofar as they are able. As a result, virtually the entire collection of colleges offers programs and instruction for them, that are apparently completed by less than half of the college-going population. The other students are pushed from the system after enrollment in institutions and programs where admission is open.

In the view then of some members of the Commission, current tests and their associated services corrupt the process of education by stultifying its development and also have the unfortunate effect of providing a rationale for its nondevelopment, since it can always be said of the unsuccessful students that they don't have what it takes—that they are not "college material." (56)

Toward the Future of Literacy Testing and the English Studies Profession

Up to this point I have assumed that literacy is the rightful business of the English studies profession—that by reproducing itself, the profession produces literacy and that that product represents English studies as an integral part of the academy. I have also assumed that the definition of literacy that emerges from English studies is closely connected with the definition of literacy that comes from standardized entrance exams in areas of "scholastic aptitude" that overlap the disciplinary boundaries of English studies. As I have tried to show, there are historical and institutional reasons for making such assumptions. The discussions and ideas that first sparked the academy's efforts to standardize a professional definition of its product originated in the early departments of English studies, newly born of the classical curriculum's legacy of rhetoric and poetic discourse. And it was men and women from English studies who led the way in a curriculum-wide process of academic professionalization through the formulation of entrance examinations as devices that defined the parameters of each department's professional turf.

Because of those conditions of origin, and an institutional lineage that links Harvard's President Eliot with the Educational Testing Service, the verbal portion of the SAT seems a perfectly reasonable site for the articulation of standards that govern English studies as an academic entity. But I now wish to propose (as indeed I have hinted already) that the historical narrative that culminates in our current understanding of academic literacy is a discontinuous text—one whose narrator changes at various turns. In these final pages I wish to consider how the agencies that define academic literacy now lie largely outside the professional auspices of those who identify themselves as English studies specialists—and how that decentering of professional definition affects our current understanding of literacy in America.

The implications, I believe, are profound. As a people we continue to look to education for cultural leadership, and that, as we have seen, is a task English studies has long identified itself as professionally prepared to undertake. But as this historical account of English studies' professional development has shown, cultural leadership as it is construed according to the liberal arts heritage of English studies is not necessarily the same as the cultural leadership demanded by the profession's academic and nonacademic clientele.

Clearly the change in demand over the past century and a half must be accounted for by the change in the college-going population itself. Initially, as we have seen, higher education and professional identity were accessible almost exclusively to those whose material conditions permitted them to contemplate culture in relatively leisurely terms. To the extent that literacy was integral to cultural leadership—or cultural production—it too could be constructed as a fairly contemplative and leisurely activity. As the working class began to change the demographics of college campuses, however, academic literacy began to take on a much more utilitarian cast—particularly as it became clear that the most direct routes to the material conditions associated with cultural leadership were through scientific and vocational curricula.

Changes in the nature of academic literacy, however, have not always resulted from the profession's determination to meet the product demands of its clientele. In fact, as we have seen in the case of entrance examinations, the standardization of professional knowledge initially undertaken from within the profession itself rapidly produced standardizing structures that have, in effect, assumed a life of their own and have arguably come to dominate the profession's own self-concept. With the introduction of the bureaucratic as well as economic influences of the Carnegie Foundation and the National Education Association to the task of standardizing college entrance requirements, responsibility for defining what Larson has termed the "cognitive domain" of the academic professions essentially left the hands of academic personnel and was appropriated by an external administrative entity, ETS.

One of the most serious consequences of that loss of professional autonomy for English studies has been the development of a confusing and contradictory relationship between the discipline's philosophies of pedagogy—its definition from within—and assessment—its definition from without. As the history of literacy assessment in the form of college entrance examinations attests, the widening of a "great gulf" (to use the terminology of Edward White) between the pedagogy and assessment of literacy has primarily been a function of the bureaucratization that inevitably accompanies centralization of authority. But as the history of literacy assessment at the college entry level also makes clear, the bureaucracy that now appears to loom outside and apart from the professional community of English studies or any other academic department was in its inception a product of academic professionalization, most notably as it took shape within emerging departments of English studies.

Directly addressing the problem of literacy assessment's estrangement from pedagogy, White urges teachers to reclaim assessment as an integral part of their repertoire of pedagogical procedures and provides considerable guidance toward such an end. In light of this historical account's demonstration of the shaping influence of assessment on curricula and pedagogy through the widespread practice of "teaching to the test," White's insistence that "testing not only can be but should be a vital part of every writing teacher's professional equipment" (2) certainly seems justified.

But despite the guidance and encouragement of English studies assessment specialists such as White, certain institutional structures currently in place as a result of the developments chronicled in the preceding chapters of this book pose formidible obstacles to progress toward literacy pedagogy's reappropriation of literacy assessment.

The fate of the proposed Portfolio Assessment Plan for the college entrance-level measurement of literacy skills illustrates the extent to which the bureaucratic structure's primary regard for time- and cost-effectiveness and for the reliability—or reproducibility—of assessment measures dominates procedural decisions made at influential sites of educational standardization.

Developed at ETS during the early 1980s, the writing portfolio project was ultimately rejected as a viable plan for replacing or even supplementing current admissions testing practices, though it has since found some acceptance and application in more localized programs at various educational levels. Very briefly, the writing portfolio project was conceived by ETS personnel in response to demands from teachers that standardized tests be brought more closely in line with current pedagogical theory. It was conceived on the premise that an admissions test of writing, if it was to uphold the value of actual writing experience, should reflect the variety of kinds of writing that students are capable of producing, both in and out of the classroom. The basic plan, in other words, was to collapse the dichotomy between "literacy for life" and "literacy for school" by designating both academic and nonacademic modes and genres of writing appropriate for assessment. In addition, the plan stressed writing, and to an extent, reading, in a more naturalistic setting (occurring in the course of classroom activities, sometimes over a period of several days and sometimes even taking place outside the classroom altogether) and evaluation by someone other than hired "experts" (an introductory letter to the portfolio, for instance, was to be directed to and read by either admissions officials or prospective employers). Featured components of the portfolio collection were to include the following:

1. an introductory letter to the portfolio
2. a personal experience writing sequence prompted by a short reading passage
3. a case study project, consisting of supplied research materials and the following two assignments:
   a. an expository, persuasive paper
   b. an analysis of a persuasive letter
4. an additional piece of writing selected by the student and representing a type of writing not otherwise contained in the portfolio

Of particular interest, because they represent the most dramatic departures from the kinds of writing traditionally featured in academic examinations are the student-selected piece and the introductory letter. In the former case, students were free to select either a school-sponsored or a nonacademic piece of their own writing. The piece was to represent what students themselves considered to be a successful piece of writing, thus encouraging them to enter into the process of critical evaluation of their own literate activities rather than passively submitting to the evaluative decisions of anonymous authorities. By placing such a decision in the hands of the individual examinee, the portfolio plan formally recognized local context as a legitimate site for the development of literacy values, thereby attempting to undermine the impulse we have seen in standardized testing to credit the universal form of a standard written language while discounting literacy as a code that functions in local contexts. The proposed portfolio plan sought to even further authenticate literacy values deriving from a local context by soliciting from examinees an explanation of why they felt the chosen piece of writing to be successful and permitting such an explanation to accompany the self-selected piece of writing included in the portfolio.

But perhaps the most radical departure from traditional literacy testing procedures was the introductory letter itself. Because it was to be directed to admissions officials or prospective employers, it demanded a response with tangible, real-world results rather than an evaluative assessment of form. In writing the letter, in other words, the student could initiate an actual *transaction* with the reader. Successful completion of the transaction could mean acceptance into a chosen educational establishment or the acquisition of gainful employment, whereas unsuccessful, "nonfunctional" performance of the transaction could mean failure to accomplish those real-life goals. To be sure, an introductory letter to a writing portfolio would not likely be the single factor in such decisions, but the assignment, by incorporating the possibility that through writing students could influence those types of decisions, was intended to underscore a functional notion of literacy as an activity involving meaningful communication and real-life material consequences.

Ultimately the portfolio plan was abandoned by ETS on the basis of its failure to meet the agency's required standards of time- and cost-efficiency, scoring reliability, and the appearance of scientific objectivity. The strength of such arguments to preserve the present system's reliance upon computer-scored, standardized tests of literacy, in fact, seems to be gathering additional force at the present juncture when educational budgets are dwindling and demands for educational excellence and accountability continue to emerge from state and national levels of the government bureaucracy. These exigencies seem inevitably to create the perception of a need for more and more standardized tests and measurements that can produce evidence of success or failure on the part of students, teachers, educational programs, and schools. Certainly such developments legislate against the creation or use of expensive, time-consuming, and unabashedly "subjective" transactional measurements of literacy, despite a growing body of pedagogical theory and practices encouraging teachers to consider the functional, socially embedded aspects of literacy and to promote them in their students' learning.

The recent proliferation of "How to Pass the SAT" texts and courses signals the extent to which the culture of standardized testing has defined an "essential product of education" beyond that of the schools themselves. Although, as we have seen, there is evidence that standardized assessment procedures have in large measure imposed their own peculiar shape upon literacy education in the schools, the growing popularity of extracurricular instruction on how to take standardized tests indicates the increasing power of such tests to communicate their own particular definition directly to the public. Moreover, despite the professed resistance of a number of such extracurricular instructional programs to the definition of educational products imposed by standardized tests (a book entitled *How to Beat the SAT* comes immediately to mind), their effect is to help individuals conform to such a definition.

If resistance is to be staged then, it must originate from within the same educational system that gave birth to the standardization movement in the first place. The professional community of English studies faces a particularly difficult challenge in accepting that responsibility since, as this history has shown, the process of formulating a standardized definition of their professional product has contributed to a fragmentation of the professional community into the supposedly opposing factions of composition and literature. Jay Robinson's account of literacy in present-day departments of English reveals the seemingly irreconcilable differences between the definitions of literacy that emerge from those two separate subcommunities, neither of which seems to accord with the definition enforced by the most influential of standardized tests. Composition theory and literary theory, as Robinson's account reveals, describe a discontinuity between the profession's specialized knowledge base and its function as a dispenser of professional service. Commenting that few if any of the English departments at major research-oriented universities have welcomed or nurtured specialists in composition or reading, Robinson observes that the dominant literary specialists in those departments promote a definition of literacy directly descended from the profession's traditional concern with cultural leadership:

> English departments mean by the term literacy one particular and quite specialized thing: an easy familiarity with a certain body of texts, a particular attitude toward them, and special practices for reading texts so that they will yield the appropriate attitudes—attitudes that might lead a professor to call one student "cultured," another "urbane," and still another a "candidate for graduate school." It is literacy thus defined that English departments strive most energetically to institutionalize: through allocation of budget resources, through vigilant protection of the tenure-track and of tenure itself, through always watchful graduate admissions, through exclusive course offerings, through careful limits placed upon what counts as serious discourse in the discipline—upon what one may say and where one may safely publish. (484)

In contrast with this emphasis on reproducing itself as an exclusive professional entity—an emphasis that concentrates departmental energy on graduate rather than undergraduate education—composition continues to be infused with the pragmatic values that it acquired in the service of education's democratization toward the end of the nineteenth century. Robinson's description of literacy as it is defined by those individuals within the profession who "teach and think about reading and writing" is focused by its attention to the *uses* of literacy competencies:

Reading and writing are complexly constituted and potentially enabling competencies that develop only when they are practiced; literacy that is worthy of the name, these practitioners tell me, develops only through the productive exercise of available and developing competencies with language—through the use of such competencies in composing and comprehending texts, through the use of language to make meanings that count for something in contexts where learning and sharing what is learned counts for something. Literacy is an outcome, not a skill, and not (even) a competency. It is something that is achieved when competencies are enabled through exercise of the human capacity to make meaning. (484–85)

During the process of conducting and composing this study I have often found occasion to speculate that it is precisely this disagreement within the profession as to just what its professional product might be that has allowed the bureaucratic offshoot of its professionalization process to acquire the powerful position it now occupies. In consequence of English studies' own reluctance to confront and reconcile ideological and philosophical discrepancies within itself, and its concomitant willingness to circumvent those conflicts by surrendering literacy assessment to a separate administrative entity, the profession has lost considerable power to transform its professional values into public policy.

In order to reclaim its professional autonomy at this point, English studies must now devote itself to serious contemplation of ways in which it can reconcile the diverse traditions and influences that have contributed to the historical development of its professional identity. Ideally such a reconciliation will result in a broader, more inclusive definition of literacy as the professional product of the discipline. Robinson himself suggests that the task at hand is to forge a connection between texts and the social experiences they mediate, in short, to achieve some synthesis of formal and functional approaches to the definition of literacy. "Even great works of literature, after all, like experiences we comfortably or uncomfortably participate in and remember," he maintains, "are stories that people tell themselves to make sense of their lives. To engage in this kind of meaning-making excludes no one, no matter what their experiences, no matter what kinds of cultural frames they have constructed" (495).

To be sure, some progress toward the goal of synthesizing the separate perspectives on literacy that have arisen from the divided entity of English studies has already been made. Foremost among those whose efforts point in that direction is Myron Tuman, whose *Preface to Literacy* suggests that texts of all kinds exemplify the human capacity to employ symbols for the construction of knowledge and understanding. The symbolic nature of all texts—those categorized as literary as well as others—facilitates the unfolding of individual as well as cultural identity in what Tuman labels the "problematic" model of literacy. This model, which seeks the merger of formal and functional definitions of literacy, stands in direct opposition to the unproblematic model, which posits literacy as the simple practice of encoding and decoding authorial intent. As the preceding pages have shown, one of the most powerful agencies for promoting the unproblematic definition of literacy is the phenomenon of standardized literacy assessment. As we have seen, the historical development of this phenomenon charts a widening gap between the discipline's twofold professional responsibilities of advancing specialized knowledge and extending its services to nonprofessional constituents. Today, the preeminent influence of standardized testing on the shape of academic literacy in the public's understanding of the concept signals the need for English studies as a teaching profession to reclaim literacy from the hands of statisticians, psychometricians, and bureaucrats. The successful accomplishment of this task requires that literacy become the site where English studies at last confronts and overcomes its split personality. By examining literacy from a multiplicity of perspectives in order to reconstruct a literacy model that accounts for both reading and writing, both composition and literary specialists may begin to approach an understanding of the professional interests and talents they share with one another.

Appendix
Bibliography
Index

Appendix: Primary Sources Obtained from University and Testing Agency Archives

City College of New York

College of the City of New York, *Examinations for Admission, English*. June, 1883. Unpublished document.

"Examination Papers (English Language and Literature)," July, 1854. *Bulletin of the Free Academy* (1855), 65.

Colgate University

"Entrance Examinations," *Madison University Catalogue* (1880–1881), 42–45.

"Entrance Examinations" and "Admission by Certificate," *Madison University Catalogue* (1889–1890), 46–47.

Harvard University

Harvard University Examinations: Papers Used at the Admissions Examination. Unpublished documents. Collection includes the following years:

1874–1876
1882–1886
1887–1890
1891–1893
1894–1914

Loyola University

"Matter of Examinations," *St. Ignatius College Catalogue* (1905), 26.

Stanford University

"Admission on Examination," *Stanford University Register* (1891–1892), 26–29.

"Admission to the University," *Stanford University Register* (1910–1911), 40–46.

University of California, Berkeley

"Specimen Examination Papers, English," *University of California Bulletin.* Collection includes the following years:

1881–1882	pp. 9–11
1887	pp. 23–28
1889	pp. 27–32

"Entrance Examinations of 1891 and 1892," *University of California Admission Circular* (1893), 41–45.

"Suggestions Regarding Preparation," *University of California Admission Circular* (1893), 22–26.

Entrance Examinations (University of California, Berkeley). Collection includes the following years:

1889–1890
1902–1907
1909–1911

University of Illinois (Urbana-Champaign)

"Questions Used in the Examination of Candidates for Admission to the Illinois Industrial University in 1868," *Catalogue* (1868–1869), 28–29.

Illinois Industrial University. "Examination Questions for Honorary and Prize Scholarships for 1870." Unpublished document.

Examination for Admission (1875). Unpublished document.

University of Texas (Austin)

"Requirements for Admission. Entrance Examinations," *University of Texas Catalogue.* Collection includes the following years:

1885–1886	pp. 86–87
1887–1888	pp. 26–27
1888–1889	pp. 28–31
1889–1890	pp. 28–30
1890–1891	pp. 29–31

"Specimen Paper of Entrance Examination in English," *University of Texas Catalogue.* Collection includes the following years.

1891–1892	pp. 59–60	1897–1898	p. 149
1892–1893	pp. 15–16	1898–1899	pp. 263–265
1893–1894	pp. 16–17	1900–1901	pp. 345–347
1894–1895	p. 17	1901–1902	pp. 319–320
1895–1896	pp. 15–17	1902–1903	pp. 331–332
1896–1897	pp. 25–27	1903–1904	pp. 374–375

1904–1905 pp. 415–416	1912–1913 pp. 483–485,
1905–1906 pp. 392–393	495–496
1906–1907 pp. 408–409	1913–1914 pp. 520–523,
1907–1908 pp. 410–411	536–537
1908–1909 pp. 431–432	1914–1915 pp. 571–572
1909–1910 p. 392	1915–1916 pp. 445–446
1910–1911 pp. 417–419,	1916–1917 pp. 474–475
430–431	1917–1918 pp. 430–431
1911–1912 pp. 449–452,	1918–1919 p. 436
463–464	1919–1920 p. 439

Yale University

Examination for Admission. Unpublished documents. Collection includes the following years: (Not all exams are paginated.)

1872	Sept., 1905
1873	1905–1906 pp. 22–23
1875	1906–1907 pp. 21–23
1876	1907–1908 pp. 19–20
1877	June, 1908
1880	1908–1909 pp. 20–21
1892	1909–1910 pp. 19–20
1893	1910–1911 pp. 15–16
1894	June, 1910
1898	Sept., 1910
1900–1901	1911–1912 pp. 24–26
1901–1902	1912–1913 pp. 23–24
1902–1903	June, 1913
June, 1903	

College Board, Educational Testing Service

College Board. *Bulletin of Information.* "Sample Questions. Scholastic Aptitude Test, Verbal Section."

1947–1948 p. 10	
1950	pp. 25–27
1952–1953 pp. 22–25	
1953–1954 pp. 25–29	
1954–1955 pp. 26–29	
1955–1956 pp. 29–32	

College Board. *A Description of the College Board Scholastic Aptitude Test.* "Verbal Questions."

1956	pp. 19–43
1960–1961 pp. 14–25	
1966–1967 pp. 10–22	
1970–1971 pp. 13–23, 36–45	

Bibliography

Adams, Charles K. "Admission to College by Certificate: University of Wisconsin." *Educational Review* 6 (1893): 69–70.

Aley, Robert J. "The College and the Freshman." *School and Society* 2.1 (1915): 152–54.

American Association of Collegiate Registrars and Admissions Officers and the College Board. *Undergraduate Admissions: The Realities of Institutional Policies, Practices, and Procedures.* New York: CEEB, 1980.

Apple, Michael. "Education and Cultural Reproduction: A Critical Reassessment of Programs for Choice." *The Public School Monopoly.* Ed. Robert B. Everhart. Cambridge, MA: Ballinger, 1982.

Applebee, Arthur. "The SAT Score Decline Report." *Slate* 2 (1977): 1–3.

———. *Tradition and Reform in the Teaching of English: A History.* Urbana, IL: NCTE, 1974.

———. "Writing and Learning in School Settings." *What Writers Know: The Language, Process, and Structure of Written Discourse.* Ed. Martin Nystrand. New York: Academic Press, 1982. 365–81.

———. *Writing in the Secondary School.* Urbana, IL: NCTE, 1981.

Arbolino, Jack. "At Last: A Mystery Unfolded . . . The True Relationship Between the College Board and ETS." *College Board Review* 127 (1983): 17–20.

Aronowitz, Stanley, and Henry Giroux. *Education under Siege: The Conservative, Liberal, and Radical Debate over Schooling.* South Hadley, MA: Bergin and Garvey, 1985.

———. "Schooling, Culture, and Literacy in the Age of Broken Dreams: A Review of Bloom and Hirsch." *Harvard Educational Review* 58 (1988): 172–94.

Arons, Stephen, and Charles Lawrence III. "The Manipulation of Consciousness: A First Amendment Critique of Schooling." *The Public School Monopoly: A Critical Analysis of Education and the State in American Society.* Ed. Robert B. Everhart. Cambridge, MA: Ballinger, 1982. 225–68.

Ballou, Frank Washington. *Scales for the Measurement of English*

Composition. Harvard-Newton Bulletin 2. Cambridge, MA: Harvard UP, 1914.

Barrow, Clyde. *Universities and the Capitalist State: Corporate Liberalism and the Reconstruction of American Higher Education, 1894–1928.* Madison, WI: U of Wisconsin P, 1990.

Bereiter, Carl, and Marlena Scardamalia. "An Attainable Version of High Literacy: Approaches to Teaching for Higher-Order Skills in Reading and Writing." *Curriculum Inquiry* 17.1 (1987): 9–30.

———. The Development of Evaluative, Diagnostic, and Remedial Capabilities in Children's Composing. Unpublished ms., 1981.

Berlin, James. *Rhetoric and Reality: Writing Instruction in American Colleges, 1900–1985.* Carbondale, IL: Southern Illinois U P, 1987.

———. *Writing Instruction in Nineteenth-Century American Colleges.* Carbondale, IL: Southern Illinois UP, 1984.

Bloom, Allan. *The Closing of the American Mind.* New York: Simon, 1981.

Bollman, Thelma Anderson. "Relationship of College Entrance Requirements and Secondary School Curriculum." Diss. U of Texas, Austin, 1942.

Bowles, Frank Hamilton. *Admission to College: A Perspective for the 1960's.* New York: CEEB, 1958.

Bowles, Frank Hamilton, and R. Pearson. *Admission to College: A Program for the 1960's.* New York: CEEB, 1962.

Brandt, Deborah. *Literacy as Involvement: The Acts of Writers, Readers, and Texts.* Carbondale, IL: Southern Illinois UP, 1990.

Briggs, Le Baron Russell. "The Harvard Admission Examination in English." *Twenty Years of School and College English.* Ed. Arthur Sherman Hill, Le Baron Russell Briggs, and Byron Satterlee Hurlbut. Cambridge, MA: Harvard UP, 1896. 12–32.

Broome, Edwin Cornelius. *A Historical and Critical Discussion of College Entrance Requirements.* New York: Macmillan, 1903.

Brownstein, Samuel C., and Mitchel Weiner. *How to Prepare for College Entrance Examinations.* Woodbury, NY: Barron's Educational Series, 1964.

Camp, Roberta. Proposal for Writing Portfolio Project. Phases I and II and Progress Report for Writing Portfolio Project: Phase I. Princeton, NJ: ETS, 1982. Unpublished ms.

———. "The Writing Folder in Post-Secondary Assessment." *Directions and Misdirections in English Evaluation.* Ed. P. J. A. Evans. Ottawa: Canadian Council of Teachers of English, 1985.

Carter, Franklin. "Modern Languages in Our Higher Institutions." *Transactions of the MLA* 2 (1886): 3–21.

Carter, Michael. "The Idea of Expertise: An Exploration of Cognitive and Social Dimensions of Writing." *College Composition and Communication* 41 (1990): 265–86.

Chall, Jane S. "Literacy: Trends and Explanations." *American Education* 20 (1984): 16–22.

City College, CUNY. "Admissions." *Undergraduate Bulletin*, 1973, 10–11.

———. "A Brief History of the City College and the City University." *Undergraduate Bulletin*, 1985–87, 7–8.

———. "Requirements for Admission." *Undergraduate Bulletin*, 1969, 29–30.

———. "Undergraduate Admissions." *Undergraduate Bulletin*, 1985–87, 9–11.

Cleeton, G. U. "The Predictive Value of Certain Measures of Ability in College Freshmen." *Journal of Educational Research* 15.5 (1927): 357–70.

Coffman, George R. "Correlation Between High School and College English." *English Journal* 11.3 (1922): 129–30.

College Board. *10 SAT's*. New York: CEEB, 1986.

College Conference on English in the Central Atlantic States. "Second Annual Report." *English Journal* 3 (1914): 189–92.

College Entrance Examination Board. *Bulletin of Information*. New York: CEEB, 1945–46.

———. *Bulletin of Information*. New York: CEEB, 1947–48.

———. *Bulletin of Information*. New York: CEEB, 1952–53.

———. *Bulletin of Information*. New York: CEEB, 1955–56.

———. *Bulletin of Information*. New York: CEEB, 1958.

———. *Entrance Examination Questions: 1901*. Boston: Ginn, 1901.

———. *Entrance Examination Questions: 1902*. Boston: Ginn, 1902.

———. *Entrance Examination Questions: 1903*. Boston: Ginn, 1903.

———. *Entrance Examination Questions: 1904*. Boston: Ginn, 1904.

———. *Entrance Examination Questions: 1905*. Boston: Ginn, 1905.

———. *Entrance Examination Questions: 1906*. Boston: Ginn, 1906.

———. *Entrance Examination Questions: 1907*. Boston: Ginn, 1907.

————. *Entrance Examination Questions: 1908.* Boston: Ginn, 1908.

————. *Entrance Examination Questions: 1909.* Boston: Ginn, 1909.

————. *Entrance Examination Questions: 1910.* Boston: Ginn, 1910.

————. *Entrance Examination Questions: 1911.* Boston: Ginn, 1911.

————. *Entrance Examination Questions: 1912.* Boston: Ginn, 1912.

————. *Entrance Examination Questions: 1913.* Boston: Ginn, 1913.

————. *Entrance Examination Questions: 1914.* Boston: Ginn, 1914.

————. *Entrance Examination Questions: 1915.* Boston: Ginn, 1915.

————. *Entrance Examination Questions: 1918.* Boston: Ginn, 1918.

————. *Entrance Examination Questions: 1921.* Boston: Ginn, 1921.

————. *Entrance Examination Questions: 1924.* Boston: Ginn, 1924.

————. *Entrance Examination Questions: 1925.* Boston: Ginn, 1925.

————. *Entrance Examination Questions: 1926.* Boston: Ginn, 1926.

————. *The Work of the College Entrance Examination Board, 1901–1925.* Boston: Ginn, 1926.

Commission on English. *Examining the Examination in English: A Report to the College Entrance Examination Board.* Cambridge, MA: Harvard UP, 1931.

Commission on English Curriculum, NCTE. "Essentials for English: A Document for Reflection and Dialogue." *College English* 45.2 (1983): 184–89.

Commission on Tests, College Entrance Examination Board. "Functions and Criticisms of College Board Tests." *Critical Issues in Testing.* Ed. Ralph Winfred Tyler and Richard M. Wolf. Berkeley: McCutchan, 1974. 54–57.

————. "The Importance of College Entrance Testing." *Critical Issues in Testing.* Ed. Ralph Winfred Tyler and Richard M. Wolf. Berkeley: McCutchan, 1974. 50–53.

Conlan, Gertrude. "Objective Measures of Writing Ability." *Writing Assessment: Issues and Strategies.* Ed. Karen L. Greenberg, Harvey S. Wiener and Richard A. Donovan. New York: Longman, 1986. 109–25.

Cook-Gumperz, Jenny. "Literacy and Schooling." *The Social Construction of Literacy.* Cambridge: Cambridge UP, 1986. 16–44.

Copperman, Paul. *The Literacy Hoax: The Decline of Reading, Writing, and Learning in the Public Schools and What We Can Do About It.* New York: Morrow, 1978.

Coy, E. W. "Admission to College by Certificate: Hughes High School, Cincinnati." *Educational Review* 6 (1983): 70–73.

Cross, Allen. "Weighing the Scales." *English Journal* 6 (1917): 183–91.

Crossley, M. L. "Factors Contributing to Poor Work in College." *School and Society* 4 (1916): 925–55.

Davis, Horace. "The Limitations of State Universities." *Educational Review* 1 (1891): 426–37.

Dobrin, David. *Writing and Technique.* Urbana, IL: NCTE, 1989.

Donlan, Thomas F. *Technical Handbook for the Scholastic Aptitude Achievement Tests.* New York: CEEB, 1984.

Dressel, Paul L., et al. *Evaluation in Higher Education.* Boston: Houghton, 1961.

Duffus, Robert. *Democracy Enters College.* New York: Scribner's, 1936.

Duffy, G., and L. R. Rochler. "The Illusion of Instruction." *Reading Research Quarterly* 17 (1982): 438–45.

Eckland, Bruce Kent. "College Entrance Examination Trends." *The Rise and Fall of National Test Scores.* Ed. Gilbert R. Austin and Herbert Garber. New York: Academic Press, 1982.

Edgeworth, F. Y. "The Statistics of Examinations." *Journal of the Royal Statistical Society* 51 (1888): 599–635.

Educational Equality Project. *Academic Preparation for College: What Students Need to Know and Be Able to Do.* New York: CEEB, 1983.

Educational Testing Service. *How the Essay in the College Board English Composition Test Is Scored: An Introduction to the Reading for Readers.* Princeton, NJ: ETS, 1978.

Eliot, Charles W. "A National University." Report made by Charles W. Eliot, President of Harvard University, to the National Educational Association (Dept. of Higher Instruction) Aug. 5, 1873. Cambridge, MA: C. W. Sever, 1874.

———. "What Has Been Gained in Uniformity of College Admissions Requirements in the Past Twenty Years?" *School Review* 12 (1904): 757–58.

Falk, Julia S. "Language Acquisition and the Teaching and Learning of Writing." *College English* 41.4 (1979): 436–47.

Farr, Roger, and Jill Edwards Olshavsky. "Is Minimum Competency Testing the Appropriate Response to the SAT Decline?" *Phi Delta Kappan* 61 (1980): 528–30.

Farrand, Wilson. "A Brief History of the College Entrance Examination Board." *The Work of the College Entrance Examination Board*. Boston: Ginn, 1926. 21–30.

———. "English in the Preparatory Schools." Association of Colleges and Preparatory Schools of the Middle States and Maryland. *Proceedings*. 99–105.

———. "The Public School and the College." *School and Society* 1.15 (1915): 505–10.

Fine, Benjamin. *Admission to American Colleges: A Study in Current Policy and Practice*. New York: Harper, 1946.

Florio, Susan, and Christopher Clark. "The Functions of Writing in an Elementary Classroom." *Research in the Teaching of English* 16 (1982): 115–30.

Flower, Linda, and John Hayes. "A Cognitive Process Theory of Writing." *College Composition and Communication* 32 (1981): 365–86.

Forbes, Roger H. "Functional Literacy and Writing: Some Cautions about Interpretation." *The Rise and Fall of National Test Scores*. Ed. Gilbert R. Austin and Herbert Garber. New York: Academic Press, 1982. 51–82.

Freed, Richard C., and Glenn J. Broadhead. "Discourse Communities, Sacred Texts, and Institutional Norms." *College Composition and Communication* 38.2 (1987): 154–65.

Freire, Paulo. *Pedagogy of the Oppressed*. Trans. M. Bergman Ramos. New York: Herder, 1970.

Fuess, Claude M. *The College Board: Its First Fifty Years*. New York: Columbia UP, 1950.

Galtung, Johan. "Literacy, Education, and Schooling—For What?" *Literacy and Social Development in the West: A Reader*. Ed. Harvey Graff. Cambridge: Cambridge UP, 1981. 271–285.

Garvey, Joseph E. *Testing for College Admissions: Trends and Issues*. Arlington, VA: Educational Research Service, 1981.

Geiger, Roger L. *To Advance Knowledge: The Growth of American Research Universities, 1900–1940*. New York: Oxford, 1986.

Godshalk, Fred I., Frances Swineford, and William Coffman. *The Measurement of Writing Ability*. New York: CEEB, 1966.

Goody, Jack. *The Domestication of the Savage Mind*. Cambridge: Cambridge UP, 1977.

Goody, Jack, and Ian Watt. "The Consequences of Literacy." *Comparative Studies in Society and History* 5 (1963): 304–45.

Gordon, Edmond W. "Toward a Qualitative Approach to Assessment." *Critical Issues in Testing*. Ed. Ralph Winfred Tyler and Richard M. Wolf. Berkeley: McCutchan, 1974. 58–62.

Graff, Gerald. *Professing Literature: An Institutional History*. Chicago: U of Chicago P, 1987.

Graff, Harvey J. *Literacy and Social Development in the West*. Cambridge: Cambridge UP, 1981.

———. "Whither the History of Literacy? The Future of the Past." *Communication* 11 (1988): 5–22.

Greenough, Chester N. "The New Plan of Admission in English to Harvard College." *English Journal* 1 (1912): 364–74.

"Growing Illiteracy of American Boys." *The Nation* 63 (1896): 284–85.

Gunther, Charles. "My Experience with the Hillegas Scale." *English Journal* 8 (1919): 535–42.

Guth, William W. "The Latin Entrance Requirement." *School and Society* 3 (1916): 701–705.

Harris, William T. "The Committee of Ten on Secondary Schools." *Educational Review* 7 (1894): 1–10.

Harste, Jerome C., Virginia Woodward, and Carolyn L. Burke. "Examining Our Assumptions: A Transactional View of Literacy and Learning." *Research in the Teaching of English* 18 (1984): 84–108.

Harvard University. *Twenty Years of School and College English*. Cambridge, MA: Harvard UP, 1896.

Haskins, Charles. *The Rise of Universities*. Ithaca, NY: Cornell UP, 1957.

Havelock, Eric A. *The Literate Revolution in Greece and its Cultural Consequences*. Princeton, NJ: Princeton UP, 1982.

———. *Preface to Plato*. Cambridge, MA: Harvard UP, 1963.

Hays, Edna. *College Entrance Requirements in English: Their Effects on the High Schools*. New York: Teachers College, Columbia UP, 1936.

Heath, Shirley Brice. "Being Illiterate in America: A Sociohistoric Perspective." *Issues in Literacy: A Research Perspective*. Ed. J. A.

Niles and R. V. Lalik. Rochester, NY: National Reading Conference, 1985. 1–18.

———. "Functions and Uses of Literacy." *Journal of Communication* 30.1 (1980): 123–33.

———. *Ways with Words: Language, Life, and Work in Communities and Classrooms.* Cambridge: Cambridge UP, 1983.

———. "What No Bedtime Story Means: Narrative Skills at Home and at School." *Language in Society* 11 (1983): 49–76.

Hill, Arthur Sherman. "An Answer to the Cry for More English." *Twenty Years of School and College English.* Ed. A. Sherman Hill, Le Baron Russell Briggs, and Byron Satterlee Hurlbut. Cambridge, MA: Harvard UP, 1896. 6–16.

Hillegas, Milo B. "A Scale for the Measurement of English Composition by Young People." *Teachers College Record* 13 (1912): 331–84.

Hirsch, E. D. "Cultural Literacy." *American Scholar* 52 (1983): 159–69.

———. *Cultural Literacy: What Every American Needs to Know.* Boston: Houghton, 1987.

———. " 'English' and the Perils of Formalism." *American Scholar* 53 (1984): 369–77.

Hoffmann, Banesh. *The Tyranny of Testing.* Westport, CT: Greenwood, 1962.

Hosic, James Fleming. "The Influence of the Uniform Entrance Requirements in English: A Brief Chapter with a Summary of Facts So Far Obtained by a Committee of the NEA and a List of References." *English Journal* 1 (1912): 95–121.

———. "The National Council of Teachers of English." *English Journal* 10 (1921): 1–10.

———. *Reorganization of English in Secondary Schools.* Bureau of Education Bulletin 2. Washington D.C.: Bureau of Education, 1917.

Hunter, Charles St. John, and David Harman. *Adult Literacy in the United States.* New York: McGraw, 1979.

Huppe, Bernard Felix, and Jack Kaminsky. *Logic and Language.* New York: Knopf, 1956.

Jencks, Christopher, and James Crouse. "Should We Relabel the SAT . . . Or Replace It?" *Measurement, Guidance, and Program Improvement: Proceedings of the 1981 ETS Invitational Conference.* Ed. William Benton Schrader. San Francisco: Jossey-Bass, 1982. 33–49.

Jorgenson, Albert Nils. "College For Everyone?" *College Admissions*. New York: CEEB, 1957. xi–xiv.

Kaestle, Carl F. "Literacy and Mainstream Culture in American History." *Language Arts* 58 (1981): 207–18.

Katz, Michael. "Critical Literacy: A Conception of Education as a Moral Right and Social Ideal." *The Public School Monopoly*. Ed. Robert B. Everhart. Cambridge, MA: Ballinger, 1982.

Kellicott, William E. "College Entrance Requirements and College Standards." *School and Society* 2 (1915): 29–36.

Kellogg, Martin. "Admission to College by Certificate." *Educational Review* 5 (1893): 384–88.

Klein, Arthur J. "Higher Education." *Biennial Survey of Education*. Bureau of Education Bulletin 25. Washington D.C.: Bureau of Education, 1928.

Klitgaard, Robert. *Choosing Elites*. New York: Basic Books, 1985.

Kozol, Jonathan. *Illiterate America*. Garden City, NY: Doubleday, 1985.

Kretovics, Joseph R. "Critical Literacy: Challenging the Assumptions of Mainstream Educational Theory." *Journal of Education* 167.2 (1985): 50–62.

Kurani, Habib Amin. *Selecting the College Student in America*. New York: Teachers College, Columbia UP, 1931.

Langer, Judith. "Literacy in American Schools: Problems and Perspectives." *American Journal of Education* 93 (1984): 107–32.

Lanham, Richard. *Literacy and the Survival of Humanism*. New Haven, CT: Yale UP, 1983.

Larson, Magoli Sarfatti. *The Rise of Professionalism: A Sociological Analysis*. Berkeley: U of California P, 1977.

Lathrop, H. B. "Entrance Examination in English at Stanford." *Educational Review* 6 (1893): 289–95.

Leonard, Arthur Wells. "Report of the Proceedings of the National Conference on Uniform Entrance Requirements." *English Journal* 1 (1912): 294–301.

Levine, David O. *The American College and the Culture of Aspiration, 1915–1940*. Ithaca, NY: Cornell UP, 1986.

Levine, Kenneth. "Functional Literacy: Fond Illusions and False Economies." *Harvard Educational Review* 52 (1982): 249–66.

Lloyd-Jones, Richard. "A Perspective on Rhetoric." *Writing: The Nature, Development, and Teaching of Written Communication*. Ed. Charles Frederikson, Marcia Farr Whiteman, and J. Dominic. Hillsdale, NJ: Lawrence J. Erlbaum Associates, 1982. 169–78.

Loret, Peter G. *A History of the Content of the Scholastic Aptitude Test.* Princeton, NJ: ETS, 1960.

Lunsford, Andrea. "The Past—and Future—of Writing Assessment." *Writing Assessment: Issues and Strategies.* Ed. Karen Greenberg, Harvey S. Wiener, and Richard A. Donovan. New York: Longman, 1986. 1–12.

Mann, Horace. "Boston Grammar and Writing Schools." *The Common School Journal* 7 (1845): 321–68.

———. "The Support of Schools: The Highest Municipal Interest." *The Common School Journal* 1 (1939): 49–56.

Marvin, Carolyn. "Attributes of Authority: Literacy Tests and the Logic of Strategic Conduct." *Communication* 11 (1988): 63–82.

Maslow, Jonathan. "Mississippi: Literate at Last." *Atlantic* 266.2 (Aug. 1990): 28–33.

McCall, W. A. "A New Kind of School Examination." *Journal of Educational Research* 1 (1920): 33–46.

McLuhan, Marshall. *Understanding Media: The Extensions of Man.* New York: McGraw, 1964.

Miller, Susan. "What Does It Mean to Be Able to Write? The Question of Writing in the Discourses of Literature and Composition." *College English* 45 (1983): 219–35.

Mischler, Elliot G. "Meaning in Context: Is There Any Other Kind?" *Harvard Educational Review* 49 (1979): 1–20.

Monroe, Walter Scott. *Written Examinations and Their Improvement.* Bureau of Educational Research, College of Education Bulletin 9. Urbana, IL: University of Illinois, 1922.

Monroe, Walter Scott, and L. B. Sounders. *The Present Status of Written Examinations and Suggestions for Their Improvement.* Bureau of Educational Research, College of Education Bulletin 17. Urbana, IL: University of Illinois, 1923.

Morris, Edgar C. "College Conference on English in the Central Atlantic States." *English Journal* 3 (1914): 189–92.

Nairn, Allan, et al. *The Reign of ETS: The Corporation That Makes Up Minds.* Ralph Nader Report on the ETS, 1980.

National Assessment of Educational Progress. *Literacy: Profiles of America's Young Adults.* Princeton, NJ: ETS Publication, Report 16-PL–02, 1985.

National Commission on Excellence in Education. *A Nation at Risk:*

The Imperative for Educational Reform. Washington D.C.: U.S. Government Printing Office, 1983.

National Council of Teachers of English. "Proceedings of the 11th Annual Meeting." *English Journal* 11 (1922): 38–50.

National Education Association. *Report of the Committee of Ten on Secondary School Studies.* New York: American Book Company for the NEA, 1894.

———. *Report of the Committee on College Entrance Requirements.* Chicago: U of Chicago P, 1899.

National Society for the Study of Education. *Intelligence: Its Nature and Nurture.* Bloomington, IL: Public School, 1940.

New England Association of Teachers of English. "Report of the Standing Committee on Entrance Requirements." *School Review* 16 (1908): 646–59.

Nicholson, Frank W. "The National Conference Committee on Standards of Colleges and Secondary Schools." *School and Society* 3 (1916): 793–94.

Nightingale, Augustus Frederick. *Handbook of Requirements for Admission to Colleges of the United States.* New York: Appleton, 1879.

Northrup, Cyrus. "Admission to College by Certificate." *Educational Review* 5 (1893): 187–88.

Noyes, Ernest C. "Progress in Standardizing the Measurement of Composition." *English Journal* 1 (1912): 532–36.

Nystrand, Martin. "Rhetoric's 'Audience' and Linguistics' 'Speech Community': Implications for Understanding Writing, Reading, and Text." *What Writers Know: The Language, Process, and Structure of Written Discourse.* Ed. Martin Nystrand. New York: Academic Press, 1982. 1–30.

Odell, Charles Watters. "Are College Students a Select Group?" Bureau of Educational Research, College of Education Bulletin 34. Urbana, IL: University of Illinois, 1927.

Ohmann, Richard. "The Decline in Literacy Is a Fiction If Not a Hoax." *Chronicle of Higher Education* 25 Oct. 1976: 32.

———. *English in America: A Radical View of the Profession.* New York: Oxford UP, 1976.

Olson, David. "From Utterance to Text: The Bias of Language in Speech and Writing." *Harvard Educational Review* 47 (1977): 257–81.

———. "On Language and Literacy." *International Journal of Psycholinguistics* 7 (1980): 69–83.

Ong, Walter. *Interfaces of the Word*. Ithaca, NY: Cornell UP, 1977.
———. *Orality and Literacy: The Technologizing of the Word*. New York: Methuen, 1982.
———. "The Writer's Audience Is Always a Fiction." *PMLA* 9 (1977): 9–21.
Osgood, Charles. "No Set Requirement of English Composition in the Freshman Year." *English Journal* 4 (1915): 231–35.
Owen, David. *None of the Above: Behind the Myth of Scholastic Aptitude*. Boston: Houghton, 1985.
———. "The SAT and Social Stratification." *Journal of Education* 168.1 (1986): 81–92.
Pancoast, Henry S. "College Entrance Requirements in English." *Educational Review* 3 (1892): 132–44.
Parker, William Riley. "Where Do English Departments Come From?" *College English* 28 (1967): 337–51.
Parry, Millman. *The Collected Papers of Millman Parry*. Ed. Adam Parry. Oxford: Oxford UP, 1971.
Paterson, Donald. "Do New and Old Type Examinations Measure Different Mental Functions?" *School and Society* 24 (1926): 246–48.
Pattison, Robert. *On Literacy*. Oxford: Oxford UP, 1982.
Payne, William Morton. *English in American Universities*. Boston: Heath, 1910.
Pierson, George Wilson. *Yale College: An Educational History 1871–1921*. New Haven, CT: Yale UP, 1952.
Pixton, William H. "A Contemporary Dilemma: The Question of Standard English." *College Composition and Communication* 25 (1974): 247–53.
Proctor, W. M., and H. Ward. "Relation of General Intelligence to the Persistence of Educational and Vocational Plans of High School Pupils." *Journal of Educational Research* 7 (1923): 277–88.
Quellmalz, Edys S. "Toward Successful Large-Scale Writing Assessment: Where Are We Now? Where Do We Go from Here?" *Educational Measurement* 3 (1984): 29–32.
Rapeer, Louis W. "College Entrance Requirements: The Judgment of Educators." *School and Society* 3 (1916): 45–59.
Ravitch, Diane. "The Continuing Crisis: Fashions in Education." *American Scholar* 53 (1984): 183–93.
Resnick, David, and Lauren Resnick. "The Nature of Literacy: An Historical Exploration." *Harvard Educational Review* 47 (1977): 370–85.

Robinson, Jay. "Literacy in the Department of English." *College English* 47 (1985): 482–98.

Russell, James E. "College Entrance Requirements." *School Review* 5 (1897): 336–37.

———. "College Entrance Requirements in English." *Educational Review* 3 (1892): 74–77.

Salmon, Lucy M. "Different Methods of Admission to College." *Educational Review* 6 (1893): 223–41.

Sanoff, Alvin P., and Lucia Solorzano. "It's at Home Where Our Language Is in Distress." *U.S. News and World Report* 18 Feb. 1985: 54–57.

Scardamalia, Marlena, and Carl Bereiter. "The Development of Evaluative, Diagnostic, and Remedial Capabilities in Children's Composing." *The Psychology of Written Language: A Developmental Approach*. Ed. Margaret Martlew. London: Wiley, 1982.

Scardamalia, Marlena, Carl Bereiter, and H. Goelman. "The Role of Production Factors in Writing Ability." *What Writers Know: The Language, Process, and Structure of Written Discourse*. Ed. Martin Nystrand. New York: Academic Press, 1982. 173–210.

Schaull, Richard. Foreword. *Pedagogy of the Oppressed*. By Paulo Freire. New York: Herder, 1970. 9–15.

Schrader, William Benton. *Distribution of SAT Scores to Colleges as an Indicator of Changes in the SAT Candidate Population*. Princeton, NJ: CEEB, 1977.

Scott, Fred Newton. "College Entrance Requirements in English. *School Review* 9 (1901): 365–78.

———. "What the West Wants in Preparatory English." *School Review* 17 (1909): 10–20.

Scribner, Sylvia. "Literacy in Three Metaphors." *American Journal of Education* 93 (1984): 365–78

Scribner, Sylvia, and Michael Cole. "Literacy Without Schooling." *Harvard Educational Review* 48 (1978): 448–61.

———. *The Psychology of Literacy*. Cambridge, MA: Harvard UP, 1981.

Shiels, Merrill. "Why Johnny Can't Write." *Newsweek* 8 Dec. 1975: 58–65.

Slack, Warner, and Douglas Porter. "The Scholastic Aptitude Test: A Critical Appraisal." *Harvard Educational Review* 50 (1980): 154–75.

Sleman, Emily F. "A Progressive Step in the Higher Education of Women." *School and Society* 4 (1916): 772–75.

Smallwood, Mary Lovett. *An Historical Study of Examinations and Grading Systems in Early American Universities.* Cambridge, MA: Harvard UP, 1935.

Snow, Catherine. "Literacy and Language: Relationships During the Preschool Years." *Harvard Educational Review* 53 (1983): 165–88.

Snow, Richard E. "Aptitude and Achievement." *Measuring Achievement: Progress over a Decade.* Ed. William Benton Schrader. San Francisco: Josey Bass, 1980. 30–59.

Soltow, Lee, and Edward Stevens. *The Rise of Literacy in the United States: A Socioeconomic Analysis to 1870.* Chicago: U of Chicago P, 1981.

St. John, C. W. *Educational Achievement in Relation to Intelligence.* Cambridge, MA: Harvard UP, 1930.

Stallard, Charles K. "Writing Readiness: A Developmental View." *Language Arts* 54 (1977): 775–79.

Stalnaker, John M. "The Essay Type of Examination." *Educational Measurement.* Ed. E. F. Lindquist. Washington, D.C.: American Council on Education, 1951. 495–530.

"Standard Tests for College Admission." *English Journal* 8 (1919): 393.

Steel, James H., and John Talman. *The Marking of Compositions.* London: Nisbet, 1936.

Stein, Nancy. "Critical Issues in the Development of Literacy Education: Toward a Theory of Learning and Instruction." *American Journal of Education* 93 (1984): 171–99.

———. "Introduction: The Development of Literacy in the American Schools." *American Journal of Education* 93 (1984): 1–5.

Steiner, George. *After Babel.* Oxford: Oxford UP, 1975.

Stephens, William Richard, and William van Til. *Education in American Life.* Boston: Houghton, 1972.

Stevens, Edward. "Illiterate Americans and 19th-Century Courts: The Meanings of Literacy." *Literacy in Historical Perspective.* Ed. Daniel Philip Resnick. Washington D.C.: Library of Congress, 1983. 59–84.

Steves, Harrison R. "High School English and College English." *English Journal* 6 (1917): 146–55.

Stricker, Frank. "American Professors in the Progressive Era: Incomes, Aspirations, and Professionalism." *Journal of Interdisciplinary History* 19 (1988): 231–57.

———. "Economic Success and Academic Professionalism: Questions from Two Decades of U.S. History (1908–1929)." *Social Science History* 12 (1988): 143–70.

Szwed, John F. "The Ethnography of Literacy." *Writing: The Nature, Development, and Teaching of Written Communication*, vol. 1. Ed. Marcia Farr Whiteman. Hillsdale, NJ: Lawrence Erlbaum, 1981. 13–23.

Taber, Sylvia Read. "Current Definitions of Literacy." *Journal of Reading* 30 (1987): 458–61.

Talbert, E. L. "Proposed Changes in the Requirements for Admission to the University of Cincinnati." *School and Society* 3 (1916): 569–70.

Tannen, Deborah. "Oral and Literate Strategies in Spoken and Written Discourse." *Literacy for Life: The Demand for Reading and Writing*. Ed. Richard Bailey and Robin Melanie Fosheim. New York: MLA, 1983. 79–96.

Thomas, Charles S. "The English Course in the High School: The New England View." *English Journal* 1 (1912): 84–94.

Thorndike, Edward L. "Notes on the Significance and Use of the Hillegas Scale for Measuring the Quality of English Composition." *English Journal* 3 (1913): 551–61.

———. "On the New Plan of Admitting Students at Columbia University." *Journal of Educational Research* 4 (1921): 95–101.

Tieje, R. E., E. G. Sutcliffe, H. N. Hillenbrand, and H. Buchen. "Systematizing Grading in Freshman Composition at a Large University." *English Journal* 4 (1915): 586–97.

Tuman, Myron. "From Astor Place to Kenyon Road: The NCTE and the Origin of English Studies." *College English* 48 (1986): 339–49.

———. *Preface to Literacy: An Inquiry into Pedagogy, Practice, and Progress*. Tuscaloosa: U of Alabama P, 1987.

Uhl, W. L. "Report of the Philadelphia Council Meeting." *English Journal* 16 (1927): 40–69.

Verne, E. "Literacy and Industrialization—The Dispossession of Speech." *Literacy and Social Development in the West*. Ed. Harvey J. Graff. Cambridge: Cambridge UP, 1981. 286–303.

Vygotsky, Lev. *Thought and Language*. Trans. Eugenia Hanfmann and Gertrude Vakar. Cambridge, MA: MIT Press, 1962.

Walters, Keith, Beth Daniell, and Mary Trachsel. "Formal and Functional Approaches to Literacy." *Language Arts* 64 (1987): 855–68.

Ward, C. H. "The Scale Illusion." *English Journal* 6 (1917): 221–30.

Watson, Goodwin Barbour. "The Specific Techniques of Investigation: Testing Intelligence, Aptitudes, and Personality." *The Scientific Movement in Education, Part 2.* Ed. National Society for the Study of Education. Bloomington, IL: Public School, 1938. 357–73.

Wellborn, Stanley. "Ahead: A Nation of Illiterates." *U.S. News and World Report.* 17 May 1982: 53–56.

White, Edward M. *Teaching and Assessing Writing.* San Francisco: Josey Bass, 1985.

Wiley, Mary Callum. "The English Examination." *English Journal* 7 (1918): 327–30.

Winterowd, W. Ross. *The Culture and Politics of Literacy.* New York: Oxford, 1989.

Witte, Stephen P., Mary Trachsel, and Keith Walters. "Literacy and the Direct Assessment of Writing: A Diachronic Perspective." *Writing Assessment: Issues and Strategies.* Ed. Karen Greenberg, Harvey Wiener, Richard Donovan. White Plains, NY: Longman, 1986. 13–33.

Woods, William F. "Nineteenth-Century Psychology and the Teaching of Writing." *College Composition and Communication* 36 (1985): 20–41.

Wooley, Edwin C. "Admission to Freshman English in the University." *English Journal* 3 (1914): 238–44.

———. "On the New Plan of Admitting Students to Columbia University." *Journal of Educational Research* 4 (1921): 95–101.

Index

MARY TRACHSEL is an assistant professor of rhetoric at the University of Iowa. She has taught composition for a number of years and is the author of several articles on literacy and testing. Her current research interests are twofold, focusing on the academic institution's valuation of maternal thinking as an epistemological process and on the concept of literacy in the field of music.